TECHNICAL
REPORT

T0306640

Targeting the Occupational Skill Pairings Needed in New Air Force Colonels

S. Craig Moore, Brent Thomas, Raymond E. Conley

Prepared for the United States Air Force

Approved for public release; distribution unlimited

RAND PROJECT AIR FORCE

The research described in this report was sponsored by the United States Air Force under Contract FA7014-06-C-0001. Further information may be obtained from the Strategic Planning Division, Directorate of Plans, Hq USAF.

Library of Congress Control Number: 2010927928

ISBN: 978-0-8330-4931-5

Published 2010 by the RAND Corporation
1776 Main Street, P.O. Box 2138, Santa Monica, CA 90407-2138
1200 South Hayes Street, Arlington, VA 22202-5050
4570 Fifth Avenue, Suite 600, Pittsburgh, PA 15213-2665
RAND URL: http://www.rand.org/
To order RAND documents or to obtain additional information, contact
Distribution Services: Telephone: (310) 451-7002;
Fax: (310) 451-6915; Email: order@rand.org

Preface

This research extends to colonels the kind of analysis reported earlier for the much smaller force of Air Force general officers (GOs) and Senior Executive Service (SES) civilians.[1] Specifically, it explains how leader requirements were identified at the colonel level and how initial ranges were established for the mixes of paired skills to be developed in field-grade officers before they are promoted to colonel. It establishes planning goals intended to help steer Air Force development teams as they guided selected officers from numerous career fields into paired skills (or secondary occupations) to gain competencies as majors and lieutenant colonels that would be important for their potential future jobs as colonels and generals. The development of those goals and a complementary approach for developing officers within their career fields were outlined at an introductory level in a previous monograph.[2] This technical report should interest Air Force functional managers, officer career-field managers, officer development teams, assignment teams, individual officers, and those creating and managing the development frameworks for civilians, enlisted personnel, and the reserve components. This material should also interest those in the Office of the Secretary of Defense and the other services who are working to develop, apply, or improve competency-based systems for managing manpower, personnel, and training.

The research was sponsored by Lt Gen Roger A. Brady, Deputy Chief of Staff, Personnel, Headquarters United States Air Force (AF/A1), and performed within the Manpower, Personnel, and Training Program of RAND Project AIR FORCE for a fiscal year 2007 study, "Force Development."

After reviewing this work's methodology and proposed skill-pairing floors with several career-field managers, the Air Force promulgated the floors among its career fields' development teams in late 2005. Several Air Force development teams then added paired skills to the "developmental vectors" they had begun issuing for individual officers within their career fields, vectors that already recommended organizations (or organization levels) or schooling options for next or future assignments. At about the same time, the Air Force broke up the Air

[1] Albert A. Robbert, Steve Drezner, John E. Boon, Lawrence M. Hanser, S. Craig Moore, Lynn M. Scott, and Herbert J. Shukiar, *Integrated Planning for the Air Force Senior Leader Workforce: Background and Methods,* Santa Monica, Calif.: RAND Corporation, TR-175-AF, 2005.

[2] S. Craig Moore and Marygail K. Brauner, *Advancing the Air Force's Force-Development Initiative*, Santa Monica, Calif.: RAND Corporation, MG-545-AF, 2007. The approach for planning officer development within individual career fields goes well beyond developing occupational skill pairs and is demonstrated in Georges Vernez, S. Craig Moore, Steven C. Martino, and Jeffrey Yuen, *Improving the Development and Utilization of Air Force Space and Missile Officers*, Santa Monica, Calif.: RAND Corporation, MG-382-AF, 2006.

Force Senior Leader Management Office (AFSLMO), which had been instrumental in creating the Air Force's force-development initiative, especially its early emphasis on the development of paired skills. The development teams did not broaden or sustain for long their emphasis on paired skills, although they continued to review their officers' progress regularly and to deliberately guide their continuing development. In the meantime, the Air Staff has concentrated on the development of members' institutional rather than occupational competencies. Institutional competencies affect personal, team, and institutional leadership, applying more universally than specific occupational competencies; and they can be inculcated substantially through education and training. Paired skills are still part of the Air Force's conceptual framework for force development:[3]

> The Air Force has determined there are clearly identifiable skill requirements for Airmen who have experiences in more than one connected career area. Force development defines the occupational skill combinations and then facilitates the education, training, and assignment processes to produce a sufficient capability within the personnel inventory. Some possible occupational skill combinations for Air Force officers are illustrated . . . below:

Notional Officer Occupational Skill Combinations:

Core Skill → Enhanced with	→ Development Skill
Pilot/Navigator	Acquisition Management
Acquisition Management	Plans and Programs
Space	Plans and Programs
Fighter Pilot	Space Operations

But the development teams no longer designate occupational skills in their guidance regarding individual officers, now recommending only

> an experience level (e.g., Joint Staff, Air Staff, MAJCOM [major command], base-level, etc.), training or education opportunity (e.g., resident DE [developmental education], advanced functional training), or position type (e.g., flight commander, division chief, instructor, special duty, etc.) . . . for [an officer's] next or subsequent assignment.

In case the Air Force's force-development initiative revisits the matter of occupational competencies, potentially revising or reinvigorating its treatment of paired skills, this technical report records the previous skill-pairing guidance and explains how it was derived.

RAND Project AIR FORCE

RAND Project AIR FORCE (PAF), a division of the RAND Corporation, is the U.S. Air Force's federally funded research and development center for studies and analyses. PAF pro-

[3] U.S. Air Force, *Leadership and Force Development*, Air Force Doctrine Document (AFDD) 1-1, February 18, 2006, p. 15.

vides the Air Force with independent analyses of policy alternatives affecting the development, employment, combat readiness, and support of current and future aerospace forces. Research is conducted in four programs: Force Modernization and Employment; Manpower, Personnel, and Training; Resource Management; and Strategy and Doctrine.

Additional information about PAF is available on our website:

http://www.rand.org/paf/

Contents

Figures

Tables

Summary

Many jobs for Air Force colonels (grade O-6) and generals (grades O-7, O-8, O-9, and O-10)[1] call for officers with specific occupational backgrounds (e.g., in fighters, mobility operations, space, intelligence, logistics, communications, acquisition, or political-military affairs). But the jobs that need a particular occupational background often do not form a practical experience pyramid (e.g., fewer jobs may be suitable as first O-6 jobs than as second O-6 jobs, or fewer may be for O-7s than for O-8s). This causes the Air Force to assign officers at some experience levels to jobs that do not necessarily call for their primary occupational backgrounds. Thus, officers from, say, the bomber community may sometimes need to fill leadership jobs where prior experience in acquisition or political-military affairs would be more appropriate. Moreover, some jobs need officers with a second occupational competency (e.g., with a primary background in bombers—either pilot or navigator—plus experience in acquisition, or a primary background in intelligence plus experience in political-military affairs). Either phenomenon implies a need for the Air Force to develop a second occupational competency, or a paired skill, in some of its future colonels and generals. Prior research recommended specific combinations of primary and paired skills for most new generals.[1]

In 2003, AFSLMO issued a list of the skill pairings needed in future GOs, and the Chief of Staff of the Air Force and the Secretary of the Air Force launched a force-development initiative to actually develop those pairings and other competencies. As part of that initiative, 38 development teams (DTs) were formed in 2004 and 2005 to assess the health of their respective career fields and to deliberately guide the development of majors and lieutenants therein. In 2004, the Air Force Personnel Center (AFPC) issued guidance for a program of two-year developmental assignments (DAs) for new graduates of intermediate developmental education (IDE), largely majors, intending to help the functional communities begin developing AFSLMO's designated skill pairings in officer cohorts. But the guidance's numerical targets were vague; some were questioned sharply; and several functional communities resisted dedicating some of their manpower slots (funding) to the development of officers from other career fields. In 2005, a conference of career-field managers (CFMs) postponed implementation of the DA program until its details could be revised and properly justified.

Toward that end, personnel leaders at the Air Staff and AFPC decided to extend down to colonels the sort of analysis that had helped establish the initial targets for the mix of occupational backgrounds in new GOs. That is, they launched efforts to identify the backgrounds needed for colonels' jobs and then derive recommended mixes of primary and paired skills for most new colonels. The earlier analysis had not considered the legal, medical, and clergy

[1] Robbert et al., 2005.

portions of the GO force, only the so-called line, where officers from all other occupations compete for promotion. The effort planned for 2005 aimed to cover all officer occupations and even Air Force civilians in grade GS-15, aspiring to address colonels and GS-15s simultaneously, as had been done for military GOs and SES civilians.[2] We developed the analytic framework described in this report as part of that effort and used it with data about colonel positions' needs that were already available.[3]

Line Colonel Positions' Needs for Primary and Paired Skills

During 2002 and 2003, RAND helped experts from the functional communities, AF/A1 staff, and MAJCOMs create, review, and refine a requirements database for 2,778 colonel positions (excluding only the medical, legal, and chaplain corps); naming the primary and paired skills needed for each position; telling which positions needed officers in their first, second, or subsequent jobs as colonels; and distinguishing which were "platform jobs," positions used frequently to help prepare or test those colonels with greater chances of eventual promotion to GO. The requirements' hallmark was their flexibility. For example, 60 percent of the positions were characterized as open to more than one primary skill, including 19 percent that were open to all (any) primary skills. Five of the top ten requirements for primary skills were flexible: any, any rated, any acquisition or any finance, any operations, and mobility (including airlift and tanker pilots and navigators). (See p. 13.) Some 78 percent of the positions did not need a paired skill at all, although they were open to colonels with paired skills. Four of the top ten requirements for paired skills were flexible: none, any acquisition, any rated or any logistics, and any acquisition or any logistics. (See p. 18.) Some 96 percent of the jobs were at least somewhat flexible in their requirements for either a primary skill, a paired skill, or both. Moreover, 38 percent were judged appropriate for colonels with different levels of experience, and only 20 percent were classified as platform jobs and, hence, open essentially only to so-called "fast-track" colonels.

Shaping a Colonel Force to Meet Positions' Requirements

Retirement rates and job durations dictate experience *pyramids* for each skill-pairing's colonels. For example, more officers with a primary skill in missile operations and a paired skill in missile maintenance should be in their first jobs as colonels than in their second or more senior jobs. The size of a skill-pairing's experience pyramid generally needs to exceed the number of positions calling for that particular pairing for two or three reasons: (1) the positions that call for the pairing need a mix of experience that does not match the natural pyramid; (2) multiple qualified candidates should be available when openings occur, permitting *selectivity*; and (3) enough senior colonels must be available to become generals, who nearly all need paired

---

2 See Robbert et al., 2005.

3 AFSLMO planned and fielded a survey in 2005 to identify the occupational and other qualifications needed for Air Force colonel and GS-15 civilian positions, but the survey did not come to full fruition. We used earlier, narrower data about colonel positions to derive targets that the development teams could use promptly to help steer their skill-pairing deliberations for individual officers beginning in fall 2005.

skills. Fortunately, the position requirements' considerable flexibility could accommodate the necessary pyramids.

We created a flow model that recommends sizes for each skill-pairing's experience pyramids (one for fast-trackers[4] and one for others), the necessary annual inflows, and alignments between the positions and each pyramid's (modeled or virtual) colonels—for example, recommending that

1. officers with a primary skill as mobility pilots or navigators fill an average of four of the six positions calling for colonels
   a. in the second experience tier
   b. with any rated primary skill
   c. with a paired skill in plans and programs
2. fighter and special operations colonels split the other two such positions equally.

This example illustrates the important fact that the model does not use fair-sharing to allocate requirements among the acceptable skills.[5] Instead, the model recommends mixes of new colonels that would sustain occupational pyramids whose skills, experience, and tracks met the jobs' requirements, aiming to minimize

1. shortfalls from selectivity goals
2. numbers of new colonels with paired skills
3. differences from a mix of skills that is specified in advance[6]
4. numbers of new colonels on the fast track
5. designation of narrower skills (e.g., it favors generic rated colonels over fighter pilots insofar as possible)
6. variations in the primary skills' shares of newcomers with paired skills.

Policy parameters control targeted levels of selectivity and GO inflow as well as adherence to experience and track specifications. For example, more new colonels need a paired skill and the mix of primary skills is less flexible if the selectivity target is higher. (See pp. 38 and 39.) Each model run involves extensive mixing and matching.

Two Optimal Solutions: The Basis for FY 2006's Occupational Development Floors

Because the flow model minimizes the number of new colonels with paired skills and favors the more flexible primary and paired skills, its solutions reflect minimum average annual num-

[4] Because they are regarded as especially sensitive, we report detailed numbers for neither platform positions nor colonels on the fast track, although those dimensions were distinguished in the analysis.

[5] Fair-sharing would allocate flexible positions in predetermined ratios among the categories of eligible colonels, the ratios based on the numbers of other positions that call for those categories. For example, if 20 jobs called for Skill A, 30 for Skill B, and 25 for either A or B, fair-sharing would allocate 10 of the latter to Skill A and the other 15 to Skill B.

[6] This analysis used the mix of primary skills seen in fiscal year (FY) 2005's population of colonels as its reference mix. The model recommended deviating from that mix only to achieve objectives that were accorded higher priority (e.g., fulfilling skill and experience requirements, meeting selectivity goals, and minimizing the need for paired skills).

bers of new colonels with each specific combination of primary and paired skill, under the selected control policies. For example, at least 13 percent of the new colonels with a primary skill as fighter pilots may need a paired skill in plans and programs, 11 percent in acquisition, and 11 percent in aerospace power employment. (See p. 125.) The team that framed the officer skill development targets adopted two sets of policy parameters that generated different minimums or floors. (See p. 43.) The more demanding set generated a solution labeled *preferred* whose floors and alignments yielded higher selectivity, closer adherence to requirements for experience and track, and more colonels with the skills needed among new GOs. The solution for the less demanding parameters was labeled *marginal*. Nearly two-thirds of the entry cohort was the same in both solutions. (See pp. 45, 125–132.) The preferred solution recommended more new colonels on the fast track, more with paired skills (58 percent versus 31 percent in the marginal solution), and less occupational flexibility. (See p. 45.) Both solutions recommended paired skills for relatively more nonrated operations colonels and for relatively fewer support colonels than for rated, logistics, and acquisition/finance colonels. (See pp. 49–56.)

Although this analysis concentrated on the mixes of paired skills needed among new colonels, it also illuminated the mix of primary skills needed in the colonel force. The optimizations recommended that rated officers constitute about 34 to 41 percent of the total (down from the 47 percent seen in 2005's actual force), that logistics officers constitute about 12 to 14 percent (up from 2005's actual 10 percent), and that acquisition/finance constitute about 18 percent (up from 2005's actual 13 percent). And they recommended some shifts within broad occupational categories (e.g., larger shares for control and recovery officers within the nonrated operations category, for public affairs within the support category, and for scientific officers within the acquisition/finance category). (See pp. 65–66.)

Deriving Developmental Floors for Officer Development Teams

The recommended solutions included floors for several primary skill groups that cut across multiple Air Force development teams' career fields—for example, "pilot" cut across the combat air force (CAF), mobility air force (MAF), and special operations force (SOF) teams, and "any acquisition or any logistics" cut across several acquisition and logistics teams. Others were narrower—e.g., "fighter pilot" and "bomber pilot" were narrower than the CAF team, and "satellite command and control" and "space lift" were narrower than the space and missile operations team).

To match the DTs' boundaries, we allocated to specific teams those developmental targets that cut across multiple teams' scopes (e.g., we allocated "pilot" targets among CAF, MAF, and SOF), and we summed the floors for primary skills within a DT's scope (e.g., for the CAF we summed all floors for new fighter, bomber, and air battle manager colonels). The allocations were purposely not based on fair shares. Instead, they aimed to balance the eligible career-fields' burdens for developing paired skills. (See pp. 73–78.) If skill-pairing draws renewed interest in the future, desirably with more time and resources available for this step, we recommend that Air Force development teams eventually (1) address the more detailed primary skills (e.g., the CAF team should distinguish fighter, bomber, and air battle manager [ABM] specialists) because such colonels often cannot substitute for each other and, consequently, their development needs can differ legitimately, and (2) ascertain whether allocations are unnecessary or inappropriate. Allocations would seem unnecessary if enough officers in the eligible career-fields' cohorts already had developed the targeted paired skills, and they would seem inappropriate if more or fewer pair-building assignments were readily available within or to some of the eligible career fields). (See pp. 71–73.)

Rated Career Fields

The analysis targeted at least 24 percent of new rated colonels with paired skills (marginal solution) but preferably at least 53 percent (preferred solution). Nearly the same percentage floors were recommended for new CAF, MAF, and SOF colonels with paired skills in total. Relatively larger shares were recommended for CAF officers with paired skills in aerospace power employment and international political-military affairs, only MAF officers were recommended with a paired skill in mobility operations, and relatively larger shares were recommended for SOF officers with paired skills in plans and programs, personnel/manpower, and logistics readiness. (See pp. 78–80.)

Nonrated Operations Career Fields

The marginal and preferred cases, respectively, recommended paired skills for at least 62 percent and at least 93 percent of new colonels from these primary career fields, ranging from 0 percent for control and recovery to 100 percent for airfield operations, space/missile operations, and intelligence. Their most common paired skills were acquisition, plans/programs, aerospace power employment, and information operations. (See pp. 81–83.)

Logistics Career Fields

The marginal and preferred floors for new logistics colonels with paired skills were 29 percent and 56 percent, respectively. The numbers were somewhat different for maintenance and for logistics readiness officers. Their most common paired skills were acquisition, communications and information systems, logistics readiness (for maintenance specialists), and maintenance (for logistics readiness specialists). (See pp. 83–84.)

Support and OSI Career Fields

The paired-skill floors for these fields were 21 percent and 36 percent in the marginal and preferred cases, respectively, ranging from 0 percent for services to 86 percent for public affairs and for personnel/manpower. Their most common paired skills were plans/programs and international political-military affairs. (See pp. 84–85.)

Acquisition and Finance Career Fields

The floors for these colonels were at least 36 percent and at least 67 percent in the marginal and preferred cases, respectively, with lower percentages for finance and higher percentages for scientists. The most common paired skills were acquisition management (for scientists and developmental engineers), any acquisition (for developmental engineers and finance officers), and space satellite command and control and space lift (but neither space paired skill was recommended for finance officers). (See pp. 84, 86–87.)

Ways to Improve the Skill-Pairing Floors

A review of how DTs used, considered, or adjusted their floors from the values in this report might point the way toward improvements in the underlying data and methodology. If the Air Force puts renewed emphasis on deliberately developing paired skills in its future leaders, we recommend such a review, plus the following steps (pp. 91–92):

- Update and forecast colonel positions' requirements for skills, tracks, and experience levels.
- Update and forecast GO inflow requirements.
- Identify the requirements for GS-15 jobs and integrate the planning for skill pairings in military and civilian personnel at these grades.
- Represent learning in the flow model (i.e., some may still gain paired skills after promotion to colonel).
- Refine the estimates of behavioral parameters (e.g., retention rates and job durations).
- Reflect uncertainties in the flow analysis (e.g., uncertainties about job durations, which colonels will stay or leave, who will be promoted to GO, and time until retirement or promotion).
- Address floors in greater detail within some DTs' scopes (e.g., recognize that fighter pilots and air battle managers are not always acceptable substitutes for each other and have legitimately different needs for paired skills).
- Account for cohorts' past development and the availability of future developmental opportunities before allocating across development teams any residual needs for skill pairs.

Acknowledgments

RAND colleagues Albert Robbert, Ray Conley, John Boon, Lynn Scott, and Herbert Shukiar worked with the previous AFSLMO, the previous Developing Aerospace Leaders (DAL) Program Office, and teams of functional experts to delineate most of the colonel positions' occupational requirements. Ray Conley and AFSLMO's Lt Col Cassie Barlow worked with functional communities to complete the data; obtained MAJCOMs' reviews, additions, and recommended revisions; and integrated all necessary changes. RAND colleague Judy Mele gleaned historical personnel data supporting our flow analysis, and Manuel Carrillo helped with the modeling. In 2005, AFSLMO's Brig Gen Richard Hassan and Gwen Rutherford released the data describing the colonel positions' occupational requirements for Air Force CFMs to review. Maj Gen Tony Przybyslawski (AFPC commander) and Maj Gen Glenn Spears (Air Force Directorate of Force Management Policy, Deputy Chief of Staff for Personnel) endorsed the idea of creating skill-pairing floors using the data and analytic approach described here, and they committed staff to participate in the effort. AFSLMO's Maj Dan Gregg and Capt Paul Emslie helped formulate the personnel flow analysis, and with AF/A1P's John Park, Maj Eric Johnson, and Maj Todd Sriver and with AFPC's Col Scott Davis, Jerry Ball, Lt Col Josh Jose, Lt Col Harold Huguley, Maj Rob Ramos, Maj Jim DeHaan, Maj Matt Santoni, Capt Jeremy Sherette, and 1LT Damon Richardson, they helped frame and revise the analytic results that became the skill-pairing floors. RAND colleagues Marygail Brauner and Michael Thirtle also worked in that milieu. Lt Gen Roger Brady (AF/A1) chartered and Maj Gen Glenn Spears (Air Staff Directorate of Force Management Policy, Deputy Chief of Staff for Personnel) and John Park chaired meetings of a working group of CFMs who reviewed the cooperative effort's methodology and preliminary results, evaluated the targets' potential utility, and recommended ways to posture them for general guidance. The working group included Col Jeffrey Fraser for the rated community; Col Wayne Hudson for space and missile operations; Col John Stankowski for maintenance and logistics; Sherry Medders for public affairs; Patrick Hogan for acquisition, scientists, and engineers; and Glenda Scheiner for financial management. RAND reviewers Michael Hix and Michael Polich made important suggestions that improved the document.

Abbreviations

ABM	air battle manager (AFSC 13B)
Acq	acquisition
AEF	air expeditionary force
AF/A1	Air Force Deputy Chief of Staff for Manpower and Personnel
AF/A1P	Air Staff Directorate of Force Management Policy, Deputy Chief of Staff for Personnel
AF/DPP	Air Force Directorate of Force Management Policy, Deputy Chief of Staff for Personnel
AF/ILM	Air Force Directorate of Maintenance, Deputy Chief of Staff for Installations and Logistics
AFDD	Air Force Doctrine Document
AF/DPXF	Force Policy Division of the Air Force Directorate for Personnel Plans, Deputy Chief of Staff for Personnel
AFI	Air Force Instruction
AFLC	Air Force Learning Council
AFPC	Air Force Personnel Center
AFR	Air Force Reserve
AFS	Air Force specialty
AFSC	Air Force specialty code
AFSLMO	Air Force Senior Leader Management Office
APE	aerospace power employment
AT	assignment team (at AFPC)
C2	command and control
C2ISR	command, control, intelligence, surveillance, and reconnaissance

C4ISR	command, control, communications, computers, intelligence, surveillance, and reconnaissance
CAF	combat air force
CC	commander
CFM	career-field manager
CORONA	meeting of Air Force four-star GOs, held three times per year
DA	developmental assignment
DAL	Developing Aerospace Leaders
DE	developmental education
DPG	Air Force General Officer Management Office
DPP	Air Staff Directorate of Personnel
DPS	Air Force Senior Executive Management Office
DT	development team
E&T	education and training
EW	electronic warfare
FA	functional authority
FAC	functional account code
FAM	functional area manager
FB	fighter or bomber
FBA	fighter, bomber, or airlift
FD	force development
FDO	Force Development Office (Air Staff)
FDSO	Force Development Support Office (AFPC)
FM	functional manager
FMDC	Force Management and Development Council
FY	fiscal year
GAMS	General Algebraic Modeling System
GO	general officer
IDE	intermediate developmental education
IO	information operations
ISR	intelligence, surveillance, and reconnaissance

LP	linear programming, a form of mathematical optimization
MAF	mobility air force
MAJCOM	major command
MDS	Manpower Data System
MO	mobility operations
NAF	numbered air force
OFDP	Officer Force Development Panel
ops	operations
OSI	Office of Special Investigations
PAS	personnel accounting symbol
PME	professional military education (now DE)
pol-mil	international political-military affairs
recce	reconnaissance
RT	rated (pilot, navigator, or air battle manager)
SAF	Air Force Secretariat
SAF/AQX	Directorate of Acquisition Integration, Office of the Assistant Secretary of the Air Force (Acquisition)
SAF/FMP	Directorate for Financial Operations, Office of Financial Management and Comptroller
SAF/PAR	Requirements and Development Division, Office of Public Affairs
SECAF	Secretary of the Air Force
SES	Senior Executive Service
SOF	special operations force
sr	senior
T&E	test and evaluation
USAF	United States Air Force
XCI	Directorate for Infrastructure Delivery, Office of Warfighting Integration and Chief Information Officer

CHAPTER ONE

Introduction

When he was the Air Force's Chief of Staff in the late 1990s, General Michael Ryan found too few general officers (GOs) qualified to fill an opening as commander of a combat-oriented numbered air force (NAF). Some candidates had extensive experience in appropriate Air Force weapon systems (fighters or bombers, in that case), but most lacked critical experience in helping to plan or manage air campaigns or joint operations that would strengthen them as combat-NAF commanders. At the same time, he saw more GOs with strong backgrounds in other specialized areas, such as acquisition, than he foresaw needing to fill future openings.

Responding to his request to ascertain why this came about, RAND found that many GO jobs needed officers with substantial background in more than one area—for example, one may need a combat pilot with experience in planning the employment of aerospace power in a joint context, another may need a fighter pilot knowledgeable and experienced in acquisition, another may need an intelligence expert with experience in international political-military affairs, and another may need someone with experience in both acquisition and logistics. Moreover, some groups of GO jobs that needed officers from the same occupation did not have well-shaped grade pyramids. For example, more manpower and personnel GOs were needed at O-8 than at O-7, and more acquisition management specialists were needed at O-7 and O-9 than at O-8.[1] Consequently, to have GOs available with the right primary expertise at the right grades, at other grades some must hold jobs that do not need their primary occupational expertise. Both observations implied that many GOs should have more than one area of occupational or functional expertise—to fill either jobs outside their area of primary expertise or jobs that need more than one area of expertise. But most GOs, apparently, had grown up within their own rather specialized operational or support communities—within their *occupational stovepipes*—and, consequently, were well prepared for only the relatively few senior positions that called for those fairly specialized backgrounds. Even supposedly *generalist* GOs whose careers had revolved around their aeronautical ratings as pilots, navigators, or air battle managers (i.e., rated officers) were found to be specialized. Without deliberate development to give them broader ranges of knowledge, skills, and abilities, mismatches would persist between future generations of both rated and nonrated GOs and the jobs they would need to fill: Too few candidates would have backgrounds appropriate for some jobs, whereas more than needed would be available for others.

Preparing more future GOs with a second area of occupational expertise promised improved job performance and valuably greater selectivity—that is, more candidates would be

[1] The GO pay grades, from the bottom, are brigadier general (O-7, one-star), major general (O-8, two-star), lieutenant general (O-9, three-star), and general (O-10, four-star).

qualified and available when openings occur—plus, more leaders would be able to integrate more knowledgeably across different functional areas. The latter seemed especially important under the Air Force's emerging expeditionary posture.[2] With concurrence from the Air Force's other four-star generals (during one of their CORONA[3] meetings), General Ryan and then–Secretary of the Air Force Whitten Peters established an initiative they called Developing Aerospace Leaders (DAL) to find practical ways to develop future leaders with paired occupational skills: a *primary* skill built up over several tours (or assignments) in one occupational area and a *secondary* skill built up over, preferably, at least two tours in another occupational area chosen deliberately to help meet anticipated requirements. Both experience and training were expected in an officer's secondary occupation or paired skill.[4] The initiative's key objective was to increase the numbers of viable replacement candidates when future GO openings occur (i.e., to increase assignment selectivity). Established in 2001, the DAL initiative was renamed force development (FD) in 2003 and continues today.[5]

Air Force Doctrine Document 1-1 defines and explains the principles that guide force development.[6] Here is a key definition from its foundational doctrine statements (p. vi):

> Force development is a series of experiences and challenges, combined with education and training [giving officers] the requisite skills, knowledge, experience, and motivation to lead and execute . . . Air Force missions [by applying] the best tools, techniques, and procedures to produce a required operational capability.

Beyond giving many future senior leaders paired occupational skills, force development aims to imbue broader competencies in personal leadership (e.g., self assessment and inspiring trust),

---

2 This posture organizes deployable elements (most of the Air Force) into ten air expeditionary forces (AEFs) that rotate in pairs through cycles of preparation, deployment (or readiness to deploy), and recovery/reconstitution. Each AEF aims to offer joint force commanders about the same capabilities across a range of operational and support functions (e.g., air dominance, precision strike, transport, surveillance/reconnaissance, intelligence, communications, logistics, and medical care). AEFs promote and benefit from close planning, training, command, and management relationships across disparate functional areas at wing level and below, far more widely and lower in the organizational structure than before. (For more, see U.S. Air Force, "Case Study: General Ryan and Creation of the AEF," *Leadership and Force Development,* Air Force Doctrine Document (AFDD) 1-1, February 18, 2006, p. 62; and GlobalSecurity.org, "Aerospace Expeditionary Force (AEF), Air and Space Expeditionary Task Force (ASETF) (Formerly Air Expeditionary Force)," website, 2009.

3 CORONAs are meetings of Air Force four-star generals and are usually held two or three times per year.

4 As far as we know, the only estimate of the initiative's cost was created in about 2003 by the Air Force's DAL Program Office, which proposed a new and sizable central organization that would take over development planning and management responsibilities previously dispersed through numerous functional communities. Senior Air Force leaders rejected the proposal and directed instead that DAL's principles be *institutionalized* through existing career-field management mechanisms and at negligible added cost, to be guided substantially by the Air Force Senior Leader Management Office (AFSLMO). The opportunity costs (e.g., selected officers may forgo some depth in their primary career fields and may be less productive while learning their paired skills) were not estimated. Some leaders probably had few concerns about those costs because they saw that many officers could acquire appropriate paired skills through existing jobs (e.g., in joint organizations, the Air Staff, major command [MAJCOM] headquarters, NAFs, and acquisition offices) that also call for their primary skills, therefore not necessarily diverting them far from their occupational mainstreams.

5 Moore and Brauner also describe some historical aspects of the force-development initiative (S. Craig Moore and Marygail Brauner, *Advancing the U.S. Air Force's Force-Development Initiative,* Santa Monica, Calif.: RAND Corporation, MG-545-AF, 2007). Robbert et al. document the analytic framework used to identify developmental targets for new GOs (Albert A. Robbert, Steve Drezner, John E. Boon, Lawrence M. Hanser, S. Craig Moore, Lynn M. Scott, and Herbert J. Shukiar, *Integrated Planning for the Air Force Senior Leader Workforce: Background and Methods,* Santa Monica, Calif.: RAND Corporation, TR-175-AF, 2005).

6 U.S. Air Force, *Leadership and Force Development,* Air Force Doctrine Document (AFDD) 1-1, February 18, 2006, p. 15.

team leadership (e.g., mentoring and promoting collaboration), and institutional leadership (e.g., shaping strategy and doctrine; stewarding resources; and attracting, retaining, and developing talent), concentrating substantially at the tactical, operational, and strategic levels of responsibility, respectively.[7]

Air Force Instruction (AFI) 36-2640[8] delineates policies and defines the roles of key players in the force-development process: Deputy Chief of Staff for Personnel (AF/A1), Force Management and Development Council (FMDC), Officer Force Development Panel (OFDP), Air Force Learning Council (AFLC), functional authorities (FAs), functional managers (FMs), functional advisory councils, career-field managers (CFMs), functional area managers (FAMs), development teams (DTs),[9] advisory panels, and, at the Air Force Personnel Center (AFPC), assignment teams (ATs).[10]

In 2004, AFPC used information from AFSLMO and issued guidance to CFMs and DTs concerning a program of developmental assignments (DAs) for new graduates of intermediate developmental education (IDE, for officers at grade O-4, major), about 120 jobs that were to be reserved for two year assignments that would help officers develop deliberately paired skills. Some development teams found the guidance vague because it did not tell each DT how many officers to channel into each secondary skill. Instead, the total numbers to be assigned from each career field and into each secondary skill were specified, and the DTs were to negotiate the specific numbers for each pairing. Moreover, the host career fields (where secondary expertise was to be developed) were to dedicate authorized positions (and funding, consequently) to develop officers from (undesignated) other career fields. Some of the numerical targets were challenged; for example, more bomber officers were targeted for DAs than were even enrolled in IDE at the time. Unable to obtain satisfactory explanations for the numbers, the career-field managers elected in early 2005 to postpone the DA program's implementation. The development teams continued to assess and guide individual officers' careers, recommending assignments to organizational levels (e.g., joint staff, Air Force headquarters, or MAJCOM headquarters), schools, or position types (e.g., flight commander, instructor, or division chief). Some DTs guided officers into paired occupations for a while thereafter, but that practice has been dropped.

AFSLMO had used historical officer continuation rates to translate targets for the numbers of colonels promoted annually to brigadier general into targets for the numbers of IDE graduates going into different types of developmental assignments.[11] Rather than revising those calculations and reissuing the guidance, AFSLMO agreed with AFPC's recommendation to create floors for the numbers of new colonels (grade O-6) needed with various combinations of primary and secondary skills, that is, with various skill pairings. To be planned according to requirements for both GO and O-6 jobs, such floors were expected to guide more accurately

---

7 At different times, the Air Force has also referred to these broader competencies as *cross-functional, enduring,* or *institutional* competencies.

8 U.S. Air Force, *Executing Total Force Development,* AFI 36-2640, December 16, 2008.

9 In 2005, about 38 DTs covered the active component's officers. Each DT's minimum membership includes an FM, or a designated representative, as chair; a CFM; AFPC AT representatives; and MAJCOM representatives.

10 The 2004 version included AFSLMO, which helped create the force-development initiative, and also designated a Force Development Office (FDO) at the Air Staff and a Force Development Support Office (FDSO) at AFPC.

11 Robbert et al., 2005.

the development of career fields through the lower grades where the DTs could guide individual officers into desirable secondary or paired skills.

In mid-2005, AFSLMO launched a survey of incumbents about their O-6 positions' prerequisites, intending to develop a database that would tell far more than just the positions' needs for primary and secondary occupational skills.[12] But AFSLMO was disestablished[13] and the survey was abandoned far short of completion, so the effort to ascertain the occupational requirements for new colonels relied instead on a database that AFSLMO, the DAL Program Office, and RAND had helped develop during 2002 and 2003.[14] Chapter Two describes the steps that created that database and summarizes the occupational and experience requirements that were identified for the line colonel positions. It addresses the positions' needs for both primary and paired skills, observes that requirements for primary skills were notably more flexible than the existing authorizations, clarifies that large numbers of O-6 positions were open to officers from all career fields, notes that even more positions would be open to officers with paired skills, and summarizes the jobs' needs for prior experience in O-6 positions.

Chapter Three then describes flow modeling that helped identify and evaluate alternative shapes the line O-6 force could take while meeting those requirements. The modeling used optimization to pursue a series of policy objectives—for example, selectivity goals (multiple qualified candidates available per opening), minimum numbers with paired skills, minimum change in the occupational mix, and maximum flexibility in the recommended occupational mix—all while preserving practical experience pyramids for the primary occupations and for their pairings with secondary skills.

Chapter Four presents two solutions from the flow model that underlay the skill-pairing goals proposed for the development teams in early fiscal year (FY) 2006. The so-called *preferred* solution reflects an O-6 force that would provide greater selectivity, adhere more closely to positions' needs for prior O-6 experience and other attributes, and produce more senior colonels with the skill combinations needed among incoming general officers. The other, *marginal* solution's force would still fulfill the O-6 jobs' needs for primary and paired skills but would meet the needs for experience less closely, accept lower selectivity, etc.

The position requirements and flow modeling addressed skills in groups that did not coincide with the existing development teams' boundaries. For example, "rated" officers could come from the combat air force (CAF), mobility air force (MAF), or special operations force (SOF) communities. Chapter Five explains how we adjusted the optimization results and derived skill-pairing floors for the DTs' career fields.

Finally, Chapter Six outlines ways to improve these skill-pairing floors and summarizes this work's thematic lessons.

In a nutshell, this document explains how leader requirements were identified at the colonel level and how initial ranges were established for the mixes of paired skills to be developed in field-grade officers before they are promoted to colonel.

---

[12] The survey also addressed GS-15 positions, approximately the civilian equivalents of military colonel positions.

[13] AFSLMO's dissolution, occasioned by officer misconduct, occurred at a critical juncture and robbed the force-development initiative's impetus toward skill pairing. The previous year's roll-out of the first (but faulty) skill-pairing guidance had raised skepticism and resistance from key occupational communities, and none of the offices that absorbed portions of AFSLMO's portfolio has renewed the drive toward skill pairing.

[14] The data from 2002 and 2003 covered only the so-called line O-6 positions, not the medical, legal, and chaplain positions that the 2005 survey aimed to also cover.

CHAPTER TWO

Colonel Positions' Requirements for Occupational Skills and Experience

In 2002, at the direction of their functional managers and in response to a request from AFSLMO, 16 small panels of functional experts met in separate half-day sessions to broadly characterize the occupational backgrounds needed for Air Force colonel positions.[1] The goal was to extend to the O-6 level a previous database that delineated such requirements (and others) for about 400 GO jobs.[2] The GO database covered only so-called line positions—excluding medical, clergy, and legal positions—so the panels addressed the corresponding approximately 2,800 colonel positions. The effort addressed only the primary and secondary occupations needed for those positions because (1) that was the level of detail explicit in developmental goals identified from analyzing the more senior executive positions and (2) there were so many more O-6 jobs than GO jobs.

The following working definitions of primary and secondary occupations (or primary and paired skills, respectively) were used during the panel deliberations and subsequent reviews:

- Primary occupation: the predominant focus of an officer's career, where a high level of professional competency is gained through several tours, together with formal and on-the-job training, and the officer can integrate the occupation's contributions with those of other occupations.
- Secondary occupation: the secondary focus of an officer's career, where the officer spends a full tour (and acquires specific training or spends a second tour), learns to provide some of the occupation's contributions, and surpasses the level of understanding needed to be merely an intelligent consumer/user of the occupation's services/products.

Primary and secondary occupational requirements were captured in a coding system that used three-digit specialty codes in the Air Force's officer classification system as a point of departure but incorporated many variations from the standard codes.[3] Variations proved nec-

[1] The panels addressed jobs in these 16 categories: combat and other operations, mobility, space, intelligence, international political-military affairs, logistics, civil engineering and services, communications/information systems, manpower/personnel/training, acquisition, financial management, inspector general/force protection/special investigations, plans/programs/requirements, academic, commander, and other.

[2] About 200 of the GO jobs were in the Air Force. The Air Force shared with the other services about another 200 such high-level jobs, usually holding them only part of the time.

[3] While it is convenient and conventional to refer to designations of the qualifications needed for specific positions as "requirements," they probably more accurately represent "preferences" or "desirable qualifications." Empirical evidence is scarce about how or even whether having the designated experience(s) enhances executive job performance. The Air Force usually fills its O-6 and GO jobs even if officers must be assigned who lack some of the preferred qualifications. Means are usually available, especially in the form of expert staffs, to prevent organizational/functional failure if the assigned leaders

essary to capture flexibilities in job requirements that could not be expressed using standard specialty codes.

AFSLMO, DAL Program Office, and RAND staff members assisted the expert panels by explaining the effort's objectives, organizing lists of jobs for them to consider, suggesting sorting and coding mechanisms to use as they reviewed jobs and characterized/declared their requirements, entering those requirements into the database, helping the panels review and revise the data, and, finally, summarizing the results.[4]

Over a several-month period that stretched through much of 2003, functional managers and the MAJCOMs who "owned" the positions reviewed and revised the expert panels' designations of the jobs' primary and secondary occupational requirements. They also designated the preferred experience level(s) (i.e., which positions were appropriate as 1st, 2nd, or subsequent (*senior*) jobs[5] for colonels) and which positions were platform jobs (i.e., important for either testing or honing a colonel's potential for becoming a GO). They regarded many jobs as appropriate for more than one level or tier of experience. *Because the designations of platform jobs are regarded as especially sensitive, we do not report their full detail here, although we use it in the analysis.* We also use *track* to distinguish platform jobs (also called *fast-track* jobs) from *not-platform* jobs (also called *not-fast-track* jobs).[6] The resulting database covered 2,778 O-6 jobs and included the following, for each job:

- Details from the Air Force Manpower Data System (MDS)—for example:
  - position number
  - personnel accounting symbol (PAS) code
  - command
  - organization title
  - location
  - organization structure code
  - authorized Air Force specialty code (AFSC)
  - functional account code (FAC)

---

falter. Moreover, effective leaders often rely on other competencies (e.g., enterprise knowledge and problem-solving skills) if they lack the preferred occupational backgrounds (see Lynn M. Scott, Steve Drezner, Rachel Rue, and Jesse Reyes, *Certain Competencies May Help Offset Lack of Expertise in Senior Air Force Jobs*, Santa Monica, Calif.: RAND Corporation, RB-235-AF, 2007a; and Lynn M. Scott, Steve Drezner, Rachel Rue, and Jesse Reyes, *Compensating for Incomplete Domain Knowledge*, Santa Monica, Calif.: RAND Corporation, DB-517-AF, 2007b). Even with those provisos, we believe that the Air Force still should strive to develop and employ officers with the backgrounds that its experts declare are needed for its executive positions. Using empirical research in the private sector, Gabarro observes that "The all-purpose general manager who can be slotted into just about any organization, function, or industry exists only in management textbooks" (John J. Gabarro, *The Dynamics of Taking Charge*, Boston, Mass.: Harvard Business School Press, 1987).

[4] The panels met in May 2002 at RAND's offices in Arlington, Virginia.

[5] Some jobs are appropriate for new colonels, some need colonels who have already served in previous assignments as colonels, etc.

[6] Officers rather than jobs follow fast tracks or not, of course. Officers promoted ahead of their peers are often said to be "on a fast track," also implying that they are perceived as having greater potential for rising to senior levels, being named to attend developmental education in residence (versus completing the work by correspondence), being selected for important assignments that will test or hone their suitability and prospects for becoming senior leaders, etc. Some staff jobs and positions as commanders of certain squadrons, groups, or wings are usually filled by or even reserved for such officers and are regarded as signaling that their incumbents may be "going places." We refer to them as platform or fast-track jobs and to the officers who would nominally hold them as fast-trackers, even though they may not hold those jobs for shorter intervals. In some contexts such people are called "hi-pos," short for high-potential officers.

- incumbent's name and duty title
- required primary occupation (or a primary skill)
- required secondary occupation (or a paired skill)
- required experience level
- designation as either a platform job or not.[7]

For example, wing-commander positions at the following six bases required senior colonels[8] with primary occupation code 11F (fighter pilot) but did not require a secondary occupation, and all were regarded as platform jobs:

- Cannon Air Force Base, New Mexico
- Davis-Monthan Air Force Base, Arizona
- Eglin Air Force Base, Florida
- Hill Air Force Base, Utah
- Shaw Air Force Base, South Carolina
- Aviano Air Base, Italy.

Positions as operations group commanders (or fighter group commanders) at the following 16 bases also required colonels with primary occupation code 11F and did not require a secondary occupation, but they were regarded as appropriate second jobs for colonels, and only three were regarded as platform jobs:

- Air Force Academy, Colorado
- Aviano Air Base, Italy
- Spangdahlem Air Base, Germany
- Cannon Air Force Base, New Mexico
- Davis-Monthan Air Force Base, Arizona
- Eglin Air Force Base, Florida
- Hill Air Force Base, Utah
- Holloman Air Force Base, New Mexico
- Langley Air Force Base, Virginia
- Pope Air Force Base, North Carolina
- Shaw Air Force Base, South Carolina
- Eielson Air Force Base, Alaska
- Kadena Air Base, Japan
- Kunsan Air Base, Korea
- Misawa Air Base, Japan
- Osan Air Base, Korea.

Similar jobs at five other bases had the same occupational requirements but could accept officers in their first jobs as colonels, and four of those five were regarded as platform jobs.

As a further illustration in a different area, the Air Force Research Laboratory had positions for nine colonels with primary occupation code 63A (acquisition management) and sec-

---

[7] Some data elements were missing for some jobs.

[8] Note that some wing-commander positions were authorized for GOs rather than colonels.

ondary occupation code 61S/62E (scientist or developmental engineer). Just one of those positions required a senior colonel and was regarded as a platform job; among the other eight that were not platform jobs, four were best suited as second jobs, one as a first job, and three for any level of O-6 experience.

Overall, the Positions' Requirements Were Substantially Flexible

Table 2.1 displays the numbers of line O-6 jobs in categories distinguished by seven broad primary occupational groups,[9] eight broad secondary occupational groups, two tracks, and three experience levels or tiers. For example, (1) 678 O-6 jobs were regarded as requiring rated primary occupations, 40 of those 678 needed secondary occupations in operations support, eight of those 40 were classified as platform jobs, and five of those eight were judged appropriate as second O-6 jobs; and (2) 443 jobs required acquisition and finance primary occupations, none of the 443 required secondary occupations in operations support but 54 required them in nonrated operations, seven of those 54 were classified as platform jobs, and three of those seven were judged appropriate as jobs for senior colonels (i.e., as third or later jobs). Appendix A tabulates fully detailed requirements for primary and secondary occupational skills and experience levels but does not show how many were platform jobs.[10]

Probably the most noteworthy characteristic of the colonel jobs' requirements, even in Appendix A's detail, is their flexibility. Table 2.2 categorizes the flexibilities for the 129 different specifications of required primary skill:

- *No* means that only one occupational category was identified as acceptable—for example, 131 positions specifically required 33Y (communications and information systems officers), 122 required 21B (equipment maintenance officers), and 20 required 13SYC (missile officers).[11]
- *Limited* means that a fairly narrow range of occupations was acceptable—for example, 11 positions required 11B/12B (bomber officers), allowing 11B (bomber pilots) and 12B

---

[9] The *rated* group encompasses pilots, navigators, and air battle managers (all with AFSCs whose first character is 1); the *operations support* group (whose AFSCs begin with 16) includes foreign area, operations staff, international political-military affairs, and planning and programming officers; the *nonrated operations* group includes other specialties whose AFSCs begin with the character 1 (e.g., space/missile operations, intelligence, and weather); the logistics group includes AFSCs whose first character is 2 (e.g., munitions and missile maintenance); the *support and OSI* (Office of Special Investigations) group includes AFSCs that begin with 3 (e.g., security forces, civil engineering, communications and information systems, and personnel) and the special investigator AFSC that begins with 7; and the *acquisition and finance* group's AFSCs begin with 6 (e.g., developmental engineers, acquisition managers, and financial managers). The *other* group includes jobs the experts said could accept colonels from more than one of the other five groups. Five jobs' requirements were never specified; for completeness, our analysis carried them as having unknown occupational requirements, no particular tier requirements, and as not-platform jobs.

[10] The subtotals in Table 2.1 (e.g., Rated Total and Logistics Total) differ somewhat from their counterparts in Appendix A because we adjusted some O-6 jobs' requirements to make them compatible with those identified previously for GO jobs. See the discussion regarding Table 2.7 later in this chapter.

[11] The expert panels often used "Y" as a wild-card character when specifying the occupations needed for certain positions, as Tables 2.2 and 2.3 show. For example, 11Y (pilot) allowed 11A (airlift pilot), 11B (bomber pilot), 11F (fighter pilot), and all other AFSCs that begin with 11.

Table 2.1
Numbers of Colonel Jobs Requiring Primary and Secondary Skills in Broad Occupational Groups, by Track and Experience Level

		Required Track and Experience Level(s)														
		Fast Track (Platform Jobs)						Not Fast Track (Not-Platform Jobs)								
Required Primary Occupational Group	Required Secondary Occupational Group	1st	1st or 2nd	2nd	2nd or Senior	Senior	Subtotal	Any	1st	1st or 2nd	2nd	2nd or Senior	Senior	Subtotal	Grand Total	Platform Share, %
Rated	None	46	15	43	16	74	194	114	33	35	150	1	24	357	551	
	Family of operations		1	3		1	5	15	1		4		4	24	29	
	Rated										1			1	1	
	Nonrated operations												1	1	1	
	Operations support			5		3	8	14	2	1	10	3	2	32	40	
	Support and OSI					1	1	1			1			2	3	
	Acquisition and finance			1	2	3	6	19	6	2	13		2	42	48	
	Other	1					1	3			1			4	5	
Rated total		47	16	52	18	82	215	166	42	38	180	4	33	463	678	24
Nonrated operations	None	8		2	6	3	19	37	11	6	20	2	4	80	99	
	Family of operations	6		3		2	11	7	2		5	1	1	16	27	
	Nonrated operations	1					1		2					2	3	
	Operations support			1			1	6	6		4			16	17	
	Logistics	1				5	6		2		1		4	7	13	
	Support and OSI								1					1	1	
	Acquisition and finance	5				2	7	1	5		3		4	13	20	
	Other		2				2		2					2	4	
Nonrated operations total		21	2	6	6	12	47	51	31	6	33	3	13	137	184	7

Table 2.1—Continued

		Required Track and Experience Level(s)														
		Fast Track (Platform Jobs)						Not Fast Track (Not-Platform Jobs)								
Required Primary Occupational Group	Required Secondary Occupational Group	1st	1st or 2nd	2nd	2nd or Senior	Senior	Subtotal	Any	1st	1st or 2nd	2nd	2nd or Senior	Senior	Subtotal	Grand Total	Platform Share, %
Operations support	None							7			7			14	14	
	Operations support							1			2			3	3	
	Logistics			1			1								1	
	Other							1				1		2	2	
Operations support total				1			1	9			9	1		19	20	1
Logistics	None	30	6	4	1	6	47	36	31	16	86	3	10	182	229	
	Nonrated operations												1	1	1	
	Logistics							1			3			4	4	
	Support and OSI	3	1				4								4	
	Acquisition and finance					1	1				6			6	7	
	Other		2				2	7	1		1			9	11	
Logistics total		33	9	4	1	7	54	44	32	16	96	3	11	202	256	9
Support and OSI	None	24	1	15	4	18	62	133	42	12	97	8	22	314	376	
	Family of operations							1	1					2	2	
	Nonrated operations										1			1	1	
	Operations support	1		1	1		3	8	3		3		1	15	18	
	Support and OSI								1		1	1	2	5	5	
	Acquisition and finance												1	1	1	
	Other		2				2	1				1		2	4	
Support and OSI total		25	3	16	5	18	67	143	47	12	102	10	26	340	407	15

Table 2.1—Continued

		Required Track and Experience Level(s)														
		Fast Track (Platform Jobs)						Not Fast Track (Not-Platform Jobs)								
Required Primary Occupational Group	Required Secondary Occupational Group	1st	1st or 2nd	2nd	2nd or Senior	Senior	Subtotal	Any	1st	1st or 2nd	2nd	2nd or Senior	Senior	Subtotal	Grand Total	Platform Share, %
Acquisition and finance	None	17		2	1	11	31	83	48	6	86	1	24	248	279	
	Family of operations										1			1	1	
	Rated					1	1	2			2		1	5	6	
	Nonrated operations	3		1		3	7	6	25		10	1	5	47	54	
	Logistics										2			2	2	
	Support and OSI				2		2	1	1					2	4	
	Acquisition and finance				1	1	2	8	8		15		2	33	35	
	Other	1		1	2	8	12	5	5	1	18	1	20	50	62	
Acquisition and finance total		21		4	6	24	55	105	87	7	134	3	52	388	443	16
Other	None	26	19	22	8	26	101	160	54	49	141	60	62	526	627	
	Family of operations	1		1		2	4	7	9		2			18	22	
	Nonrated operations	1		2	3		6	10	1	6	7		7	31	37	
	Operations support	2		4		2	8	18	8	1	10	1	4	42	50	
	Support and OSI	1	1	1		1	4	4		1	9		4	18	22	
	Acquisition and finance							9	1		4	1		15	15	
	Other					1	1	6	1		3		1	11	12	
Other total		31	20	30	11	32	124	214	74	57	176	62	78	661	785	28

Table 2.1—Continued

		Required Track and Experience Level(s)														
		Fast Track (Platform Jobs)						Not Fast Track (Not-Platform Jobs)								
Required Primary Occupational Group	Required Secondary Occupational Group	1st	1st or 2nd	2nd	2nd or Senior	Senior	Subtotal	Any	1st	1st or 2nd	2nd	2nd or Senior	Senior	Subtotal	Grand Total	Platform Share, %
Unknown	Unknown							5						5	5	
Unknown total								5						5	5	0
Grand total		178	50	113	47	175	563	737	313	136	730	86	213	2,215	2,778	20
		32%	9%	20%	8%	31%	100%	33%	14%	6%	33%	4%	10%	100%		
							20%							80%	100%	

NOTE: The secondary occupational groups in the table include one more broad category than the primary occupational groups: the *family of operations* group encompasses requirements for aerospace power employment, information operations, electronic warfare, and mobility operations.

Table 2.2
Flexibility Categories, by Required Primary Skill

Primary Code	Required Primary Skill	Flexible?	No. of Jobs
11A	Airlift pilot	No	20
11A/12A	Airlift	Limited	17
11A/12A/63A	Airlift or acquisition management	Substantial	1
11B/12B	Bomber	Limited	11
11B/12B/13SYC	Bomber or missile	Limited	15
11B/12B/3YY	Bomber or any support	Substantial	3
11E	Experimental-test pilot	No	1
11F	Fighter pilot	No	85
11F/11B	Fighter or bomber pilot	Limited	1
11F/11H	Fighter or helicopter pilot	Limited	2
11H	Helicopter pilot	No	2
11H/11S/12S	Helicopter pilot or SOF	Limited	18
11M	Mobility pilot	Limited	9
11R	Reconnaissance pilot	No	1
11S/12S	Special operations	Limited	18
11S/12S/13D	SOF or control and recovery	Limited	1
11S/12S/13DYA	SOF or control and recovery rescue	Limited	2
11S/12S/13DYB	SOF or control and recovery special tactics	Limited	1
11Y	Pilot	Substantial	42
13A	Astronaut	No	9
13B	Air battle manager (ABM)	No	4
13B/13D	ABM or control and recovery	Limited	2
13D	Control and recovery	No	1
13M	Airfield operations	No	1
13S	Space or missile	Limited	44
13S/14N	Space, missile, or intelligence	Limited	7
13S/14N/61S/62E	Space, missile, intelligence, scientist, or developmental engineering	Substantial	1
13S/62E	Space, missile, or devopmental engineering	Limited	3
13S/63A	Space, missile, or acquisition management	Limited	1
13S/6YY	Space, or missile, acquisition/financial management	Substantial	4
13SYA	Space satellite command and control (C2)	No	4
13SYA/B/D/E	Any space	Limited	3
13SYA/D/E	Space satellite C2, surveillance, or warning	Limited	1

Table 2.2—Continued

Primary Code	Required Primary Skill	Flexible?	No. of Jobs
13SYB	Space lift	No	8
13SYC	Missile	No	20
13SYD	Space surveillance	No	2
13SYD/E	Space surveillance or space warning	Limited	2
13Y	Space, missile, or C2	Substantial	1
14N	Intelligence	No	75
14N/33Y	Intelligence or communications	Limited	5
15W	Weather	No	15
16F/16P	Foreign area or international political-military affairs	Limited	2
16P	International political-military affairs	No	6
16R	Plans/programs	No	10
16R/63A	Plans/programs or acquisition management	Limited	2
1YE	Experimental-test	Limited	8
1YF	Fighter	Limited	20
1YF/13B	Fighter or ABM	Limited	4
1YF/1YM	Fighter or mobility	Substantial	1
1YM	Mobility	Limited	79
1YM/11S/12S	Mobility or SOF	Limited	1
1YM/21R	Mobility or logistics readiness	Limited	8
1YM/63A	Mobility or acquisition management	Limited	1
1YR	Reconnaissance	Limited	4
1YR/13B	Reconnaissance or ABM	Limited	3
1YT	Tanker	No	17
1YY	Any operations	Substantial	106
1YY/33Y	Any operations or communications	Substantial	14
1YY/33Y/62E	Any operations, communications, or developmental engineering	Substantial	1
1YY/62EYF	Any operations or flight test developmental engineering	Substantial	1
1YY/63A	Any operations or acquisition management	Substantial	1
21A	Aircraft maintenance	No	3
21B	Equipment maintenance	No	122
21B/21R	Equipment maintenance or logistics readiness	Limited	33
21B/63A	Equipment maintenance or acquisition management	Limited	3
21G	Logistics plans	No	9

Table 2.2—Continued

Primary Code	Required Primary Skill	Flexible?	No. of Jobs
21M	Munitions and missile maintenance	Limited	2
21MYA	Munitions and missile maintenance, missile	No	8
21MYB	Munitions and missile maintenance, spacelift	No	4
21R	Logistics readiness	No	70
21S	Supply	No	1
21T	Transportation	No	1
2YY	Any logistics	Substantial	3
2YY/63A	Any logistics or acquisition management	Substantial	2
2YY/63A/64P	Any logistics, acquisition management, or contracting	Substantial	1
31P	Security forces	No	10
31P/36P	Security forces or personnel	Limited	1
32E	Civil engineering	No	74
32E/33Y/62E/ 63A	Civil engineering, communications/information, developmental engineering, or acquisition management	Substantial	1
32E/34M	Civil engineering or services	Limited	1
33Y	Communications and information systems	No	131
33Y/63A	Communications and information or acquisition management	Limited	1
33Y/6YY	Communications and information or acquisition/financial management	Substantial	1
34M	Services	No	19
35B	Band	No	1
35P	Public affairs	No	21
36P	Personnel	No	33
36P/38M	Personnel or manpower	Limited	50
38M	Manpower	No	10
3YY	Any support	Substantial	6
60C	Program director	No	1
61S	Scientist	Limited	20
61S/62E	Scientist or developmental engineering	Limited	20
61S/62E/63A	Scientist, developmental engineering, or acquisition management	Substantial	4
61SYA	Analytical scientist	No	1
62E	Developmental engineering	No	22
62E/63A	Developmental engineering or acquisition management	Limited	2
63A	Acquisition management	No	106

Table 2.2—Continued

Primary Code	Required Primary Skill	Flexible?	No. of Jobs
64P	Contracting	No	44
65F	Financial management	No	53
65F/65W	Financial management or cost analysis	Limited	2
65W	Cost analysis	No	1
6YY	Acquisition/financial management	Substantial	124
71S	Special investigations	No	20
Acq	Any acquisition	Substantial	43
Acq/2YY	Any acquisition or any logistics	Substantial	1
Any	Any	Yes	517
APE	Aerospace power employment	No	10
FB	Fighter or bomber	Substantial	48
FB/13B	Fighter, bomber, or ABM	Substantial	3
FB/16R	Fighter, bomber, or plans/programs	Substantial	3
FB/1YM	Fighter, bomber, or mobility	Substantial	4
FB/1YM/11S/12S	Fighter, bomber, mobility, or SOF	Substantial	1
FBA	Fighter, bomber, or airlift	Substantial	40
FBA/63A	Fighter, bomber, airlift, or acquisition management	Substantial	2
IO	Information operations	No	25
IO/14N	Information operations or intelligence	Limited	1
MO	Mobility operations	No	1
RT	Any rated	Substantial	172
RT not 13B	Any rated except ABM	Substantial	33
RT/13M	Any rated or airfield operations	Substantial	3
RT/13S	Any rated, space, or missile	Substantial	2
RT/13Y	Any rated, space, missile, or C2	Substantial	30
RT/13Y/14N	Any rated, space, missile, C2, or intelligence	Substantial	2
RT/14N	Any rated or intelligence	Substantial	1
RT/21G	Any rated or logistics plans	Substantial	1
RT/APE	any rated or aerospace power employment	Substantial	1
RT/IO	Any rated or information operations	Substantial	5
Unknown	Unknown	No	5
Grand total			2,778

(bomber navigators), 15 required 11B/12B/13SYC (bomber or missile officers), and 20 required 61S/62E (scientist or developmental engineering officers).
- *Substantial* means that a wider range of occupations was allowed—for example, 172 positions required RT (rated officers), allowing 11Y (pilots), 12Y (navigators), and 13B (air battle managers); 124 required 6YY (acquisition/financial management officers), allowing 61S (scientists), 62E (developmental engineers), 63A (acquisition managers), 64P (contracting), 65A (auditing), 65F (financial managers), and 65W (cost analysis); and 48 required FB (fighter or bomber officers), including both pilots and navigators.
- *Yes* means that all occupations were allowed.

Some 1,661 jobs (60 percent) exhibited at least limited flexibility in their requirements for primary occupations, including the 517 jobs (19 percent) that could accept officers from any primary occupational specialty.[12] Five of the top ten requirements for primary skills were flexible: Any (any), RT (any rated), 6YY (acquisition/financial management), 1YY (any operations), and 1YM (mobility, including airlift and tanker pilots and navigators). The other five were not flexible: 33Y (communications and information systems), 21B (equipment maintenance), 63A (acquisition management), 11F (fighter pilot), and 14N (intelligence).

Similarly, Table 2.3 categorizes the flexibilities for the 70 different specifications of a required secondary or paired skill. The jobs that exhibited at least limited flexibility in these requirements (2,427 jobs, 87 percent), included 2,175 jobs (78 percent) that needed no secondary occupation at all. Of the 603 jobs (22 percent) that needed secondary occupations, about four out of ten could accept more than one secondary occupation. Four of the top ten requirements for secondary skills were flexible: None (none), Acq (any acquisition), RT/2YY (any rated or any logistics), and Acq/2YY (any acquisition or any logistics). The other six were not flexible: 16R (plans/programs), APE (aerospace power employment), 16P (international political-military affairs), 14N (intelligence), IO (information operations), and 63A (acquisition management).

Appendix A lists the 303 combinations of primary and secondary skills that were required. Because only 22 percent of the positions required secondary skills, the most common requirements specified only primary skills. Table 2.4 lists the top ten combinations that required secondary skills. Among the table's 165 positions, the primary and secondary skill requirements were completely specific for only 12: those requiring 14N (intelligence) primary and IO (information operations) secondary.

Figure 2.1 summarizes flexibilities in the pairs of required primary and secondary skills. Requirements for secondary skills were notably more flexible than for primary skills. Summarized further into four major categories:

- Only 98 jobs (4 percent) were completely specific in both their primary and secondary occupational requirements—for example, 11 jobs required 13SYC (missile) officers with secondary skill 21MYA (missile maintenance).
- 1,019 (37 percent) were specific in their primary requirements but at least somewhat flexible in their secondary requirements—for example, 11 required 63A (acquisition manager) with secondary skill 61S/62E (scientist or developmental engineer).

[12] Because the expert panels did not consider the medical, legal, or chaplain specialties, it is unclear whether these 517 jobs could accept colonels from those occupations.

Table 2.3
Flexibility Categories, by Required Secondary Skill

Secondary Code	Required Secondary Skill	Flexible?	No. of Jobs
11B	Bomber pilot	No	1
11S/12S	Special operations	Limited	1
13B	Air battle manager	No	2
13B/13S/36P	ABM space, missile, or personnel	Limited	1
13B/D/M	Command, control, intelligence, surveillance, and reconnaissance (C2ISR)	Limited	1
13S	Space or missile	Limited	17
13S/14N	Space, missile, or intelligence	Limited	4
13S/15W	Space, missile, or weather	Limited	2
13S/62E	Space, missile, or developmental engineering	Limited	1
13S/63A	Space, missile, or acquisition management	Limited	1
13SYA	Space satellite C2	No	10
13SYA/15W	Space satellite C2 or weather	Limited	1
13SYA/B/D/E	Any space	Limited	4
13SYA/E	Space satellite C2 or space warning	Limited	2
13SYB	Space lift	No	9
13SYB/C	Space lift or missile	Limited	3
13SYB/C/21M	Space lift, missile, or munitions and missile maintenance	Limited	1
13SYC	Missile	No	2
13SYC/21M	Missile or munitions and missile maintenance	Limited	1
13SYD	Space surveillance	No	1
13SYD/E	Space surveillance or space warning	Limited	5
13SYE	Space warning	No	2
14N	Intelligence	No	34
14N/33Y	Intelligence or communications/information systems	Limited	1
16F	Foreign area	No	2
16F/16P	Foreign area or international political-mililitary affairs	Limited	2
16P	International political-military affairs	No	41
16R	Plans/programs	No	83
16R/21R/33Y	Plans/programs, logistics readiness, or communications/information	Substantial	1
1YM/63A	Mobility or acquisition management	Limited	1
1YR/14N	Reconnaissance or intelligence	Limited	2
1YY	Any operations	Substantial	5

Table 2.3—Continued

Secondary Code	Required Secondary Skill	Flexible?	No. of Jobs
1YY/21A	Any operations or aircraft maintenance	Substantial	7
1YY/2YY	Any operations or any logistics	Substantial	2
1YY/65F/65W	Any operations, financial management, or cost analysis	Substantial	1
1YY/65Y	Any operations or finance	Substantial	1
21M	Munitions and missile maintenance	Limited	2
21MYA	Munitions and missile maintenance, missile	No	12
21T/34M/81T	Transportation, services, or education and training	Limited	1
2YY	Any logistics	Substantial	6
2YY/63A	Any logistics or acquisition management	Substantial	1
32E	Civil engineering	No	2
33Y	Communications and information systems	No	16
36P	Personnel	No	15
36P/38M	Personnel or manpower	Limited	5
3YY	Any support	Substantial	1
61S	Scientist	No	2
61S/62E	Scientist or developmental engineering	Limited	11
62E	Developmental engineering	Limited	2
62EYF	Flight test developmental engineering	No	1
63A	Acquisition management	No	23
65F	Financial management	No	1
6YY	Acquisition/financial management	Substantial	16
81T	Education and training	No	6
86M/86P	Operations management or command and control	Limited	1
Acq	Any acquisition	Substantial	69
Acq/21M	Any acquisition or munitions and missile maintenance	Substantial	1
Acq/2YY	Any acquisition or any logistics	Substantial	18
Acq/62E	Any acquisition or developmental engineering	Substantial	1
Any	Any	Yes	2
APE	Aerospace power employment	No	43
EW	Electronic warfare	No	1
IO	Information operations	No	34
IO/62E	information operations or developmental engineering	Limited	1
MO	Mobility operations	No	3

Table 2.3—Continued

Secondary Code	Required Secondary Skill	Flexible?	No. of Jobs
None	None	Yes	2,175
RT not 13B	Any rated except ABM	Substantial	3
RT/21M	Any rated or munitions and missile maintenance	Substantial	4
RT/2YY	Any rated or any logistics	Substantial	39
Unknown	Unknown	No	5
Grand total			2,778

Table 2.4
Top Ten Occupational Requirements That Included a Secondary Skill

Primary Skill			Secondary Skill			No. of Jobs
Required Code and Skill		Flexible?	Required Code and Skill		Flexible?	
63A	Acquisition management	No	RT/2YY	Any rated or any logistics	Substantial	39
RT	Any rated	Substantial	16R	Plans/programs	No	23
Any	Any	Yes	16P	International political-military affairs	No	16
61S/62E	Scientist or developmental engineering	Limited	63A	Acquisition management	No	13
Any	Any	Yes	14N	Intelligence	No	13
FB	Fighter or bomber	Substantial	Acq	Any acquisition	Substantial	13
14N	Intelligence	No	IO	Information operations	No	12
1YY	Any operations	Substantial	14N	Intelligence	No	12
1YY/33Y	Any operations or communications/information systems	Substantial	IO	Information operations	No	12
RT	Any rated	Substantial	APE	Aerospace power employment	No	12

- 253 (9 percent) were at least somewhat flexible in their primary requirements but specific in their secondary requirements—for example, 23 required RT (any rated occupation) as the primary skill but 16R (plans/programs) as the specific secondary skill.
- 1,408 (51 percent) were at least somewhat flexible in both their primary and secondary occupational requirements—for example, 13 required either fighter or bomber pilots or navigators with any acquisition occupation[13] as the secondary skill.

In total, 2,680 (96 percent) of the jobs were at least somewhat flexible in their requirements for either primary occupation, secondary occupation, or both.

[13] The acquisition occupations include 61S (scientist), 62E (developmental engineer), 63A (acquisition management), and 64P (contracting).

Figure 2.1
Requirements for Secondary Skills Are More Flexible Than for Primary Skills

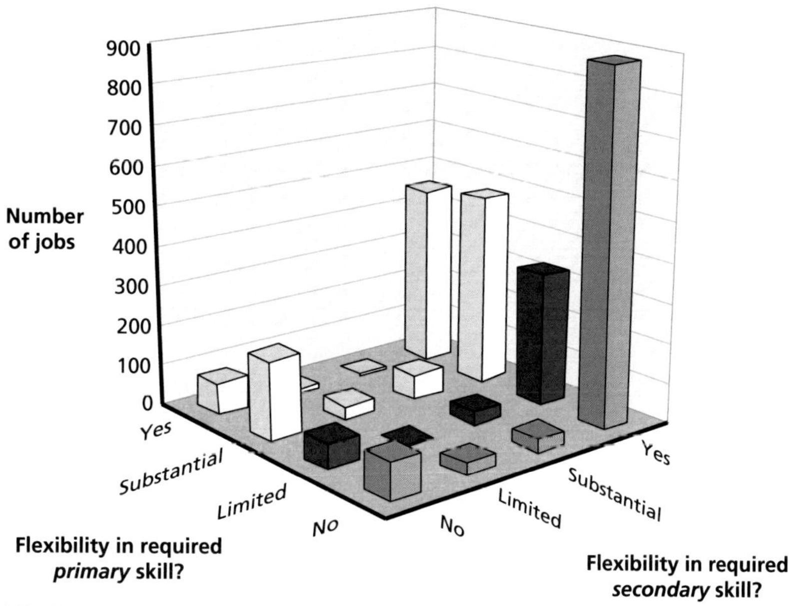

RAND *TR759-2.1*

The jobs were also considerably flexible in their requirements for experience (recall Table 2.1): 1,056 (38 percent) jobs were judged appropriate for colonels with different levels of experience, including 737 (27 percent) open to any experience level. Because jobs not characterizedas platform jobs generally can be filled by colonels whether or not they are regarded as on a fast track, 80 percent of the positions were flexible in that respect.

All told, only 24 (0.9 percent) of the 2,778 colonel jobs in 2002 were judged to be completely specific in their requirements for primary occupation, secondary occupation, experience level, and track. The other 99.1 percent were at least somewhat flexible in one or more of those regards.

It seems worth noting that, compared with other jobs, platform jobs tended to be somewhat

- more specific about required primary skills (61 percent had limited flexibility or none, compared with 54 percent of other jobs)
- slightly less demanding about secondary skills (19 percent required a secondary skill, compared with 22 percent of other jobs)
- slightly less specific about secondary skills (14 percent had limited flexibility or none, compared with 16 percent of other jobs)
- more specific about experience levels (83 percent were earmarked for just one experience level, compared with 57 percent of other jobs).

Many More Jobs Were Open to Each Occupation Than Were Authorized

The experts usually were less specific about primary skill requirements than were the manpower data system's authorized AFSCs. Table 2.5 illustrates the situation for two career fields: 11F (fighter pilot) and 63A (acquisition manager). The experts judged that only 15 (about 12 percent) of the 126 positions authorized for fighter pilots actually needed fighter pilots, whereas 38 (30 percent) could accept RT = any rated occupation (11Y = pilot, 12Y = navigator, or 13B = air battle manager), another 23 (18 percent) could accept FB = any fighter or bomber specialty (11F = fighter pilot, 12F = fighter navigator, 11B = bomber pilot, or 12B = bomber navigator), etc. And they judged that only 70 (about 37 percent) of the 190 positions authorized for acquisition managers specifically needed 63A as the primary occupation, whereas 73 (38 percent) could accept 6YY = acquisition/financial management = any acquisition or financial specialty, 25 (13 percent) could accept Acq = any acquisition specialty, etc.

It is worth noting in Table 2.5 that the experts thought (a) one job that was authorized 11F (fighter pilot) more appropriately required the primary occupation 11B/12B (bomber pilot or navigator), and (b) several jobs that were authorized 63A (acquisition manager) more appropriately required other primary occupations (e.g., two required 64P [contracting] and two required 1YY [any operations]). Overall, the experts regarded the authorized specialty as an inappropriate primary skill for about 3 percent of the jobs.[14] The required primary skill and the authorized specialty were the same for only about 21 percent of the jobs.

Naturally, the flexibility in the experts' designated requirements for primary occupations meant that many more jobs were open to each specialty than were specifically authorized. (We already noted that 546 jobs [20 percent] were regarded as open to all primary skills.) Table 2.6 lists the total numbers and percentages of jobs that the experts designated as open to each three-character AFSC as a primary occupation, for the AFSCs specifically authorized in FY 2002. For example, 44 percent of the O-6 jobs were designated as open to 11F (fighter pilot), 40 percent to 12A (airlift navigator), 24 percent to 32E (civil engineer), and 31 percent to 63A (acquisition manager). Notably more positions were designated as open to rated officers. Because the experts determined that experience more specific than three-character AFSCs was needed for some jobs, Table 2.6 lists at least one shredout[15] for four AFSCs: 13D, 13S, 61S, and 62E.

This report uses the experts' designations instead of formal authorizations as the numbers of jobs open to each occupational group of colonels.

---

[14] We counted only cases with clear-cut conflicts between authorized specialties and required primary occupations—for example, 11F (fighter pilot) is inappropriate against a requirement for 11B/12B (bomber pilot or navigator), and 63A (acquisition manager) is inappropriate against a requirement for 61S/62E (scientist or developmental engineer). We counted no conflicts among the 26 percent of the jobs with flexible authorized specialties, often considered "tax" jobs. For example, we regarded authorized specialties 30C (support commander), 81T (formal training instructor), and 87G (inspector general) as acceptable against a requirement for RT (any rated primary occupation), even though the requirement is more specific than the authorized specialty—because there is no inherent reason why officers in those jobs could not be rated.

[15] A shredout, shred, or suffix is the fifth character, if any, in an officer specialty code, AFSC. An AFSC's first three characters identify its career field. For example, the C shredout indicates missile crew specialists within the 13S (space and missile operations) career field.

Table 2.5
Primary Skill Requirements Often Were Less Specific Than Authorized AFSCs

Authorized AFSC	Primary Code	Required Primary Skill	No. of Jobs
11F	RT	Any rated	38
	FB	Fighter or bomber	23
	FBA	Fighter, bomber, or airlift	17
	1YY	Any operations	17
	11F	Fighter pilot	15
	11Y	Pilot	4
	RT not 13B	Any rated except ABM	3
	FB/16R	Fighter, bomber, or plans/programs	3
	1YF	Fighter	2
	Any	Any	2
	FB/1YM	Fighter, bomber, or mobility	1
	11B/12B	Bomber	1
11F total			126
63A	6YY	Acquisition/financial management	73
	63A	Acquisition management	70
	Acq	Any acquisition	25
	61S/62E	Scientist or developmental engineering	4
	13S/6YY	Space, missile, or acquisition/financial management	2
	64P	Contracting	2
	61S/62E/63A	Scientist, developmental engineering, or acquisition management	2
	1YY	Any operations	2
	RT	Any rated	1
	2YY/63A/64P	Any logistics, acquisition management, or contracting	1
	13Y	Space, missile, or C2	1
	1YY/63A	Any operations or acquisition management	1
	62E/63A	Developmental engineering or acquisition management	1
	13S/63A	Space, missile, or acquisition management	1
	1YM/63A	Mobility or acquisition management	1
	11A/12A/63A	Airlift or acquisition management	1
	1YE	Experimental-test	1
	FBA/63A	Fighter, bomber, airlift, or acquisition management	1
63A total			190

Table 2.6
Numbers of Line O-6 Jobs Open to Career Fields Authorized in FY 2002

Authorized AFSC	Description	No. and % of Open Jobs	
11A	Airlift pilot	1,179	42
11B	Bomber pilot	1,130	41
11E	Experimental-test pilot	992	36
11F	Fighter pilot	1,213	44
11G	Generalist pilot	983	35
11H	Helicopter pilot	1,014	37
11K	Trainer pilot	983	35
11R	Reconnaissance/surveillance/electronic warfare pilot	1,000	36
11S	SOF pilot	1,034	37
11T	Tanker pilot	1,116	40
12A	Airlift navigator	1,107	40
12B	Bomber navigator	1,086	39
12E	Experimental-test navigator	949	34
12F	Fighter navigator	1,082	39
12G	Generalist navigator	941	34
12R	Reconnaissance/surveillance/electronic warfare navigator	956	34
12S	SOF navigator	991	36
12T	Tanker navigator	1,064	38
13A	Astronaut	733	26
13B	Air battle manager	970	35
13D	Control and recovery	728	26
13DYA	Control and recovery, rescue	730	26
13DYB	Control and recovery, special tactics	729	26
13M	Air field operations	728	26
13S	Space and missile operations	786	28
13SYA	Space and missile operations, satellite C2	794	29
13SYB	Space and missile operations, space lift	797	29
13SYC	Space and missile operations, missile	821	30
13SYD	Space and missile operations, surveillance	794	29
13SYE	Space and missile operations, warning	792	29
14N	Intelligence	782	28
15W	Weather	706	25

Table 2.6—Continued

Authorized AFSC	Description	No. and % of Open Jobs	
21A	Aircraft maintenance	583	21
21B	Equipment maintenance	738	27
21G	Logistics plans	701	25
21L	Logistician	613	22
21R	Logistics readiness	691	25
21S	Supply	692	25
21T	Transportation	692	25
31P	Security forces	618	22
32E	Civil engineering	653	24
33S	Communications and information systems	731	26
34M	Services	597	21
35B	Band	578	21
35P	Public affairs	598	22
36P	Personnel	661	24
38M	Manpower	637	23
61S	Scientist	786	28
61SYA	Scientific analyst	787	28
62E	Developmental engineer	795	29
62EYF	Developmental engineer, flight test	796	29
63A	Acquisition management	867	31
64P	Contracting	786	28
65A	Auditing	697	25
65F	Financial management	752	27
65W	Cost analysis	700	25
71S	Special investigations	588	21
Grand total		2,788	100

Secondary Skills Paired with Primary Skills

Table 2.3 shows that the ten secondary skills required most frequently were, in order:

- 16R (plans and programs)
- Acq (any acquisition)
- APE (aerospace power employment)

- 16P (international political-military affairs)
- RT/2YY (rated or any logistics)
- IO (information operations)
- 14N (intelligence)
- 63A (acquisition management)
- Acq/2YY (any acquisition or any logistics)
- 13S (space or missile).

And Appendix A shows that the ten primary/secondary pairings required most frequently were, in order:

- 63A (acquisition manager) primary with RT/2YY (any rated or any logistics) secondary
- RT (any rated) primary with 16R (plans and programs) secondary
- Any (any) primary with 16P (international political-military affairs) secondary
- 61S/62E (scientist or developmental engineer) primary with 63A (acquisition management) secondary
- Any (any) primary with 14N (intelligence) secondary
- FB (fighter or bomber) primary with Acq (any acquisition) secondary
- 14N (intelligence) primary with IO (information operations) secondary
- 1YY (any operations) primary with 14N (intelligence) secondary
- 1YY/33Y (any operations or communications) primary with IO (information operations) secondary
- RT (any rated) primary with APE (aerospace power employment) secondary.

Adjustments in the Position Requirements

We altered the experts' specifications of some requirements to maintain compatibility with those identified previously for GO and Senior Executive Service (SES) positions. Some of the primary occupations designated for O-6 positions had been regarded only as secondary occupations in the previous analyses (e.g., aerospace power employment and information operations). Conversely, some of the secondary occupations designated for O-6 positions had been regarded only as primary occupations in the previous analyses (i.e., all rated occupations). Table 2.7 lists the adjustments we made. The largest adjustment was converting 39 jobs that required acquisition manager as the primary occupation and either a rated or logistics secondary occupation to requiring either a rated or logistics primary occupation and acquisition manager as the secondary occupation. Most officers whose expertise combines acquisition management with either rated operations or logistics gain their competency in acquisition management after first becoming proficient in their rated or logistics occupations.

In a few cases, the experts apparently regarded secondary occupations as alternatives (second choices) rather than as occupations to be paired with primary occupations. For example, we interpreted a stated requirement for 32E (civil engineering) as the primary occupation and 3YY (any support) as the secondary occupation as a requirement for 32E (civil engineering) as the primary occupation, a preferred case of 3YY (any support), with no requirement for a particular secondary occupation.

Table 2.7
Adjustments in O-6 Positions' Occupational Requirements

Original		Adjusted		
Primary	**Secondary**	**Primary**	**Secondary**	**Total**
Change Nominal Secondaries from Primary to Secondary				
16F/16P	None	Any	16F/16P	2
16P	16F	Any	16F/16P	1
16P	None	Any	16P	5
16R	1YY/65F/65W	1YY/65F/65W	16R	1
16R	1YY/65Y	1YY/65Y	16R	1
16R	2YY	2YY	16R	1
16R	None	Any	16R	7
16R/63A	16P	63A	16P/16R	2
APE	IO	14N	APE/IO	2
APE	None	RT	APE	8
FB/16R	APE	FB	APE	3
IO	14N	14N	IO	3
IO	16R	1YR/13B/14N/33Y	16R	4
IO	61S	61S	IO	1
IO	Acq	1YR/13B/14N/33Y	Acq	1
IO	Acq/2YY	1YR/13B/14N/33Y	Acq/2YY	2
IO	None	Any	IO	14
IO/14N	16R	14N	16R	1
MO	None	1YM	MO	1
RT/APE	None	RT	APE	1
RT/IO	16R	1YR/13B/14N/33Y	16R	1
RT/IO	None	RT	IO	4
Change Rated Secondaries to Primaries				
1YM/63A	1YM/63A	1YM	63A	1
1YR	13B	1YR/13B	None	1
33Y	13B/13S/36P	13B/13S/33Y/36P	None	1
62E/63A	RT not 13B	RT not 13B	62E/63A	1
63A	1YR/14N	1YR/14N	63A	1
63A	1YY/2YY	1YY/2YY	63A	1
63A	RT/2YY	RT/2YY	63A	39
6YY	11B	11B	6YY	1

Table 2.7—Continued

Original		Adjusted		
Primary	**Secondary**	**Primary**	**Secondary**	**Total**
6YY	11S/12S	11S/12S	6YY	1
6YY	1YR/14N	1YR/14N	6YY	1
6YY	RT not 13B	RT not 13B	6YY	2
6YY	RT/21M	RT/21M	6YY	4
Delete Secondary Alternates				
32E	3YY	32E	None	1
60C	Acq	Acq	None	1
64P	6YY	64P	None	1
RT	1YY	RT	None	1
65F	Acq/62E	65F	Acq	1
Change 81T to E&T				
13S	81T	13S	E&T	2
14N	81T	14N	E&T	1
21B	81T	21B	E&T	2
3YY	81T	3YY	E&T	1
31P	21T/34M/81T	31P	21T/34M/E&T	1

We also changed the designation 81T to E&T to better reflect the broader need for expertise in education and training rather than specifically the need to have been a formal training instructor.

Officers with Secondary Occupations Qualify for More O-6 Positions

Because the primary skill requirements were substantially flexible, each primary career field was regarded as qualified to fill numerous colonel positions, and having a secondary occupation would qualify members for even more. For example, bomber pilots with no paired skill qualified for 837 O-6 jobs, about 30 percent of the total line O-6 jobs, whereas bomber pilots with a paired skill in 63A (acquisition management) qualified for 934 jobs, or nearly 34 percent. As another example, intelligence officers with no paired skill qualified for 607, somewhat less than 22 percent, and intelligence officers with a paired skill in information operations qualified for 654, or nearly 24 percent.

Part of the original purpose for developing officers with paired skills was to make more candidates eligible for position openings at the general-officer level. Opening similar flexibility at the colonel level could also have dramatic effects. For example, if colonel bomber pilots with a paired skill in acquisition management were regarded as qualified for colonel positions that require acquisition management as the primary occupation, they would be candidates for 1,396 line O-6 positions, more than 50 percent of the 2,778 total.

Revised Requirements and the Future May Be More Demanding

It seems worth noting that the concept of paired skills was fairly new and unfamiliar when Air Force functional representatives identified the line O-6 positions' occupational requirements during FY 2002. Moreover, relatively few line colonels then had enough experience outside their primary occupations to be regarded as having developed skills to the level of a secondary occupation. Consequently, the experts may have been somewhat reluctant to register needs for paired skills. If the idea of paired skills were to take root and as paired skills became more common, however, hiring authorities might more often designate needs for secondary occupational skills.

In separate studies addressing the needs for experience, education, and training before holding different field-grade jobs in the 13S (space/missile operations), 14N (intelligence), and RT (any rated) career fields, the vast majority of O-6 positions were regarded as needing functional experience beyond officers' occupational stovepipes.[16] Those studies did not designate paired skills, secondary occupations, or associated thresholds, however, so the experts may have been less reluctant to register the need for broader experiences.

Other studies have also considered the possibility that future jobs may demand wider experience than today's. For example, the 13S study analyzed a case where all future command positions would require prior experience in both warfighting and acquisition positions, consistent with a recommendation from the government's National Security Space study.[17] Similar work (unpublished) identified and assessed potential requirements for more and new skill pairs in the future GO-level force, especially for positions that require space; command, control, communications, computers, intelligence, surveillance, and reconnaissance (C4ISR); or information operations experience. When such needs become more widely recognized, paired-skill requirements may spread to more O-6 positions.

---

[16] For 13S positions' needs, see Georges Vernez, S. Craig Moore, Steven Martino, and Jeffrey Yuen, *Improving the Development and Utilization of Air Force Space and Missile Officers*, Santa Monica, Calif.: RAND Corporation, MG-382-AF, 2006; and for 14N positions' needs, see Marygail K. Brauner, Hugh G. Massey, S. Craig Moore, and Darren Medlin, *Improving Development and Utilization of Air Force Intelligence Officers*, Santa Monica, Calif.: RAND Corporation, TR-628-AF, 2009. Results from the rated work are not published. In all three studies, experts prioritized as critical, important, or useful the positions' needs for functional skills beyond the occupations' technical stovepipes. At higher grades, relatively more jobs needed broader experience and more often the need was critical.

[17] Commission to Assess United States National Security Space Management and Organization, *Report of the Commission to Assess United States National Security Space Management and Organization,* Washington, D.C., January 11, 2001.

CHAPTER THREE

Shaping a Colonel Force to Meet Positions' Requirements

Beyond meeting the positions' needs for primary and paired skills, for prior experience as a colonel, or for fast-track officers, the colonel force must be shaped to provide suitable crops of candidates for promotion to GO and conform to practical retention and assignment patterns. Meeting these goals and others simultaneously is so complex that we needed to develop a new model to help analyze alternatives and recommend practical targets. Paralleling our findings in similar previous studies, it turns out that notably more people than jobs need paired skills. In this chapter, we first describe an extreme case that illustrates this need and then address the needs for paired skills among new GOs, which the force of colonels should routinely graduate. Then we outline the colonel-level flow model (Appendix B describes the model in more detail) and compare it with closely related models, before delineating two optimal solutions in Chapter Four.

Why More People Than Jobs Need Paired Skills

Consider an actual set of designated requirements: 11 O-6 jobs needed 13SYC (missile crew) as the primary occupation and 21MYA (munitions and missile maintenance) as the paired skill. The difficulty is that nine of the 11 jobs were designated for senior colonels (candidates with at least two previous O-6 jobs) and only one each for the first and second tiers. Moreover, five of the nine senior-tier jobs were designated for fast-track colonels, the other four were not, and the jobs in the first and second tiers were not. Obviously, more than 11 colonels were needed with this skill pairing to grow the necessary number of senior colonels. Straightforward flow analysis, applying continuation rates and average lengths of tiers (more about those parameters later), would target an inventory averaging about 31 such colonels, about 22 of them at the first and second tiers where most would need to do other jobs.[1] Providing a selectivity of at least 3.0 for openings in the senior tier would grow the total further to about 41 colonels.[2]

---

[1] Using simple formulas that will be introduced soon, and assuming the loss rates and tier lengths listed in Table 3.1, it is easy to calculate that it takes an average of about 1.7 new fast-track and 3.3 new not-fast-track colonels annually to maintain an average of 9 colonels in the senior tier, 5 of them fast-trackers. This would generate an average of about (1) 2.8 fast-track and 6.5 other colonels in the second tier, or 9.3 in total, where only one was needed, and (2) 3.3 fast-track and 9.1 other colonels in the first tier, or 12.4 in total, also where only one was needed.

[2] The average stays in the senior tier show that the Air Force could expect about 3.1 openings per year for new senior colonels, about 1.6 of them for fast-trackers. Elevating these numbers by 2.0 (as will be explained below) would target minimum selectivity of 3.0 for the nine senior-tier positions, and it would take about 6.5 new colonels per year in total, about 3.7 of them fast-trackers, to sustain that flow into the senior tier. The resulting force would average about 14.5 senior-tier, 11.7 second-tier, and 15.0 first-tier colonels, an average 41.2 in total.

This extreme case illustrates that information about positions' requirements goes only part of the way toward ascertaining developmental targets for occupational skills. Compared with this example, most requirements do not necessitate as many more people than jobs with a given occupational pairing. Nevertheless, the targeted numbers of people normally exceed the numbers of jobs, and by amounts that depend on the jobs' track and tier requirements and on the specificity of their occupational requirements.

Fortunately, the flexibility in other positions' occupational and seniority needs can accommodate many of the seemingly extra officers needed with specific occupational skills, as we will soon demonstrate.

Nearly All New Generals Need Paired Skills

In the analyses of senior officer developmental needs completed up through late FY 2005, about 88 percent of the GO jobs were regarded as needing paired skills. Flow analyses found that virtually all new GOs would need paired skills to sustain inventories of leaders at all four GO grades with skills matching the requirements reasonably closely, offering multiple qualified candidates when openings occurred, allowing sufficiently equitable promotion opportunities for officers with different combinations of skills, etc. Although a very wide range of incoming mixes of skills could provide equally workable GO forces, the share of new GOs needing paired skills remained at virtually 100 percent.

To help analyze the needs for incoming colonels with paired skills, we used minimum numbers previously identified for individual skill pairings in new GOs—for example, how many new GOs per year were needed with primary backgrounds in these pairings: fighters with a paired skill in aerospace power employment, fighters with a paired skill in acquisition, airlift with a paired skill in mobility operations, intelligence with a paired skill in information operations, logistics with a paired skill in acquisition, or acquisition management with a paired skill in developmental engineering. These minimums added to about 30, roughly 75 to 80 percent of the total average annual GO inflow. For example, the force of senior colonels should be able to generate at least about two new GOs per year with a primary background in fighters and a paired skill in international political-military affairs, nearly as many with a primary background in airlift and a paired skill in aerospace power employment, and nearly as many with a primary background in special operations and a paired skill in aerospace power employment. Some 81 different combinations of primary and paired skills had such minimums, most of them quite small. More than 50 combinations reflected minimum average annual GO inflows of less than one per four years. Here, we delineate neither the full list of pairings nor their numerical targets because the Air Force regards them as sensitive information.

Even though relatively few incoming colonels eventually become GOs, the need for a stream of new generals, properly prepared, is one driver in planning for the colonel force.

Please note that requiring, say, 90 percent confidence that selectivity would be adequate would increase the number of missile-and-maintenance colonels needed still further. Although we worked out ways to address such confidence levels, we did not use them in this exercise. Their complications were judged unnecessary for purposes of quickly establishing new developmental objectives, because they would slow the process and make it more difficult to explain.

A Flow Model for Assessing O-6 Alternatives and Recommending Targets

Appendix B contains the detailed mathematics for our O-6 flow model, which uses a steady-state analytic framework[3] and the linear programming optimization method.[4] Here we describe the model conceptually: first its fundamental variables, then practical limits (policy limits) on the variables' values, and, finally, the policy goals that lead to specific recommendations.

Fundamental Variables

The model's key decision variables are O-6 inflows and assignments:

- the average *number of new colonels* per year (1) on the fast-track versus not and (2) with each combination of primary and paired skills
- the average *number of colonels* (1) on the fast-track versus not, (2) with each combination of primary and paired skills, and (3) at each level of experience *assigned to positions* calling for each (1) track, (2) combination of primary and paired skills, and (3) level of experience.

Flows into second and senior colonel levels or tiers are modeled as proportional to initial inflows, applying the estimated loss rates shown in Table 3.1. For example, if an average of 20 officers per year were promoted to colonel, were not regarded as fast-trackers, and had primary and paired skills as fighter pilots and in aerospace power employment, respectively, then averages of 20 × 87.4 percent = 17.5 such officers per year would enter the second tier and 17.5 × 61.7 percent = 10.8 per year would enter the senior tier. Time and data limitations prevented our testing how or whether loss rates vary across populations of colonels with different occupational backgrounds.[5] Table 3.1 also shows the estimated lengths of the three experience tiers. The model uses the following relationship[6] to calculate strengths for various elements of the colonel workforce:

Average inventory = (Average inflow per year) × (Average years' stay).

Table 3.1
Estimated O-6 Loss Rates and Tier Lengths

	Fast Track		Not Fast Track	
Tier	**Loss Rate**	**Length, Years**	**Loss Rate**	**Length, Years**
Senior	—	3.10	—	2.25
Second	0.0%	1.75	38.3%	2.25
First	3.3%	2.00	12.6%	2.75

[3] Steady-state personnel models reflect long-term, self-replicating workforces: hiring, assignment, promotion, and separation patterns are the same from year to year and the workforces' average size, mix, and utilization remain unchanged.

[4] See, for example, Frederick S. Hillier and Gerald J. Lieberman, *Introduction to Operations Research,* 8th ed., New York: McGraw-Hill, 2005.

[5] Indeed, even Table 3.1's estimated values are relatively coarse; they are based on summary data that AFSLMO provided about several cohorts' continuation and eventual separation.

[6] This applies Little's Law, a result from steady-state queueing theory. See John D.C. Little, "A Proof of the Queueing Formula $L = \lambda W$," *Operations Research*, Vol. 9, 1961, pp. 383–387.

As an illustration, average annual promotions to colonel of 20 officers with a specified primary and paired skill, if the officers were not regarded as fast-trackers, would yield long-run averages of 20 × 2.75 = 55.0 such colonels in the first experience tier, 17.5 × 2.25 = 39.3 in the second experience tier, and 10.8 × 2.25 = 24.3 in the senior experience tier, averaging some 118.6 in all. In comparison, if 20 fast-trackers were promoted annually, the model would calculate averages of 20 × 2.00 = 40.0, 20 × 96.7 percent × 1.75 = 33.8, and 20 × 96.7 percent × 100 percent × 3.10 = 60.0 colonels in the first, second, and senior experience tiers, respectively, or an average of 133.8 in all.

The flow model recommends average numbers of officers to promote to colonel annually with each combination of primary and paired skill and either on a fast track or not. Together with Table 3.1's estimated values, those promotions imply an entire colonel workforce's long-run size and its mix of experience, tracks, and occupational skills. The model recommends this workforce and a way of aligning it with the colonel positions, aiming to match modeled colonels' qualifications with positions' requirements. Because the positions' requirements are quite flexible and the alternative colonel workforces are innumerable, the model uses optimization to recommend flows and assignments that would (1) satisfy practical limits and (2) maximize or minimize declared goals or objectives.

Practical (and Policy) Limits

The constraints that limit the modeled workforce's size, mix, and alignments—even if some look complicated as delineated in Appendix B's mathematical terms—are relatively straightforward conceptually:

- The total number of colonels should match the total number of colonel positions. The model reflects this limit in two steps: Assignments must (1) fill all jobs, and (2) employ the entire workforce. Moreover, the math insists that the assigned colonels meet the positions' requirements for primary and paired occupational skills.[7]
- Positions requiring fast-track colonels should be filled at least X percent of the time by such colonels.[8]
- Positions requiring colonels with a given level of experience should be filled at least Y percent of the time by such colonels.[9]

---

[7] Naturally, the model can recommend that some skill requirements be met using colonels with different backgrounds (e.g., that positions needing fighter or bomber officers should go to fighter pilots about 20 percent of the time, fighter navigators 25 percent, bomber pilots 35 percent, and bomber navigators 20 percent). It is worth reemphasizing that such recommended percentages are seldom proportional to the numbers of positions needing more-specific qualifications, whether the need is for track, level of experience, or occupational skill.

Note: The logic insists that modeled colonels' skills fulfill the positions' requirements perfectly, a luxury enabled by the extensive flexibility in positions' requirements. With less flexibility, we could have identified and prioritized the permissible imperfect matches, as in earlier analysis of stocks, flows, and utilization of the executive workforce of GOs and SES members (Robbert et al., 2005).

[8] AFSLMO staff thought that the experts' designations of fast-track requirements were too weak to warrant strict enforcement. We examined the solution's sensitivity to the track designations by varying the parameter X. The greater that percentage, the closer the model must adhere to the stated fast-track requirements.

[9] AFSLMO staff also thought that the experts' designations of experience requirements did not warrant strict enforcement. We examined the solution's sensitivity to these designations by varying the parameter Y. The greater that percentage, the closer the model must adhere to the stated experience requirements.

- The average numbers of colonels leaving the senior tier annually must meet the requirements for new generals. This constraint is also implemented in two steps: For each combination of primary and paired skill needed for the GO force, (1) enough senior colonels must become available in total,[10] and (2) enough of them must be fast-track colonels.[11]
- Multiple colonels from the appropriate track(s), with targeted experience, and with appropriate primary and paired skills must be available for each vacancy. Users can specify the desired level for minimum selectivity—that is, how many appropriate candidates should be available, on average, for vacancies.[12]

The principal complexity in expressing these constraints mathematically is that most of the requirements are open to many categories of colonels. Table 3.2 displays the combinations of track and experience level allowed to meet the various requirements for track and experience. In the table "Part" means that the column's colonels can meet some but not all of the row's requirements. For example, users may tell the model that at least, say, 90 percent of the positions calling for fast-track colonels in their second jobs must be filled by such colonels, allowing up to 10 percent of the positions to be filled either by senior colonels or first-tier, fast-track colonels. Appendix C tells how the extensive combinations of primary and paired skills were recognized that meet the various forms of occupational requirements (e.g., 95 different combinations can meet a requirement for rated officers, and 33 can meet a requirement for logistics officers, whereas only one can meet a requirement for a primary skill as a fighter pilot with a paired skill in aerospace power employment, and only one can meet a requirement for maintenance as the primary skill with acquisition management as the paired skill).

Policy Goals That Lead to Recommendations

Most readers probably remember solving simultaneous algebraic equations in school (e.g., "two equations in two unknowns"). Planning the colonel force is fundamentally akin to those problems, except (1) there are many more equations and unknowns, (2) many of the relationships are inequalities instead of equations, and (3) there are many more unknowns (variables) than equations and inequalities. The differences imply that the planning problem has no unique solution: multitudes of different settings for the variables can satisfy all of the inequalities and equations. To help the flow model recommend good settings for the variables, we seek values that would optimize objectives that aim to facilitate force management and development:

---

[10] Model users can readily specify that the colonel force generate a multiple of the minimum GO inflows per year (e.g., to see the effects of requiring that an average of twice as many colonels as needed become available for promotion to GO). The more GO candidates demanded, the greater the GO inflow's influence on the mix of incoming colonels.

[11] Users can specify the minimum fraction of GOs that must come from fast-track colonels. The greater that minimum, the stronger the influence of the GO force requirements on the mix of incoming fast-track colonels.

[12] For example, providing two more candidates than the expected number of vacancies would yield minimum average selectivity of three. To illustrate: If an average of five vacancies were expected per year for second-tier colonel positions that required some combination of primary and paired skills, then a pool of seven qualified candidates graduating from first-tier positions would yield minimum selectivity of three: Seven candidates would be available for the first of the seven openings, six candidates for the second, five for the third, four for the fourth, and three for the fifth.

Table 3.2
Matching Track and Experience Requirements

Required by Jobs		Acceptable Colonel Inventory		
Track	**Experience Level**	**1st**	**2nd**	**Senior**
		Fast Track		
Fast	1st	All	Part	
	1st or 2nd	All	All	Part
	2nd	Part	All	Part
	2nd or senior	Part	All	All
	Senior		Part	All
	Any	All	All	All
Fast or not	1st	All	Part	
	1st or 2nd	All	All	Part
	2nd	Part	All	Part
	2nd or senior	Part	All	All
	Senior		Part	All
	Any	All	All	All
		Not Fast Track		
Fast	1st	Part	Part	
	1st or 2nd	Part	Part	
	2nd		Part	Part
	2nd or senior		Part	Part
	Senior			Part
	Any	Part	Part	Part
Fast or not	1st	All	Part	
	1st or 2nd	All	All	Part
	2nd	Part	All	Part
	2nd or senior	Part	All	All
	Senior		Part	All
	Any	All	All	All

- Minimize the worst shortfall in selectivity. If it proves impossible to provide selectivity as high as sought for some positions, recommend how to keep it as high as possible in the lowest case.

- Minimize the overall shortfall in selectivity. If it proves impossible to provide selectivity as high as sought for multiple categories of positions, recommend how to keep it as high as possible for the worst-off positions in each such category.
- Minimize the number of new colonels with paired skills. Although it is perfectly acceptable to promote more new colonels with paired skills, knowing the smallest workable numbers can help planners target the minimum development needed during grades O-5 and lower.
- Minimize the differences between the recommended incoming cohort's mix of primary skills and a mix proposed judgmentally (e.g., one based on the skill mix of O-5 positions, previous cohorts promoted to O-6, or the current O-6 mix). This goal keeps the model from recommending changes from expectations or past practice unless they are necessary to meet other goals or constraints.
- Minimize the number of new colonels on the fast track, who are regarded as likely candidates for promotion to GO.
- Maximize flexibility in the skills targeted for new cohorts of colonels. For example, recommend as many new colonels as possible in the primary skill categories listed earlier in the following series and as few as necessary in those listed later: *Any, Any Operations, Any Rated, Fighter or Bomber, Bomber, Bomber Pilot.* Do the same for the following list of paired skills: *None, Any, Any Acquisition, Acquisition Management.* The model should recommend skill categories as loosely as possible. Any real promotion cohort will be more specific, of course, but the idea here is to allow as many different mixes as possible: Do not make the floors more specific than necessary.[13]
- Minimize variations across the primary skills' recommended fractions of new colonels with paired skills. This objective aims to even the career fields' burdens in developing paired skills.

The model is guided further by the priorities accorded these objectives. It optimizes one objective at a time, each time without degrading the solution's performance on any objective receiving a higher priority. Changing the priorities will usually change the final optimization solution. For the purposes of establishing developmental floors, the objectives were prioritized in the order in which they are listed above.

Solutions are also affected by key parameter settings. Figure 3.1 illustrates how three parameter settings affect the share of new colonels who need a secondary or a paired skill: If the selectivity target is higher, if more of the requirements for experience are to be met, and if more of the requirements for fast-track colonels are to be met, then more new colonels need a paired skill. For example, at the low end, only about 23 percent of the new colonels would need a paired skill if the selectivity target were 1.0 (at least one qualified candidate per opening) and if the requirements for properly experienced and for fast-track colonels were ignored. At the high end, about 54 percent of new colonels would need paired skills if the selectivity target were 3.0 and if the requirements for experience and for fast-track colonels were to be met

[13] This avoids fair-sharing or other arbitrary allocation rules at this stage, and it specifies the recommended mix of new colonels as flexibly as possible. Although individual officers have specific skills, such as 11F (fighter pilot), 12B (bomber navigator), or 13B (air battle manager), those and many additional occupations stay available to force managers and promotion boards if the optimization can recommend the undifferentiated RT (rated) category instead.

Figure 3.1
How Parameter Settings Affect the Minimum Share of New Colonels Needing Paired Skills

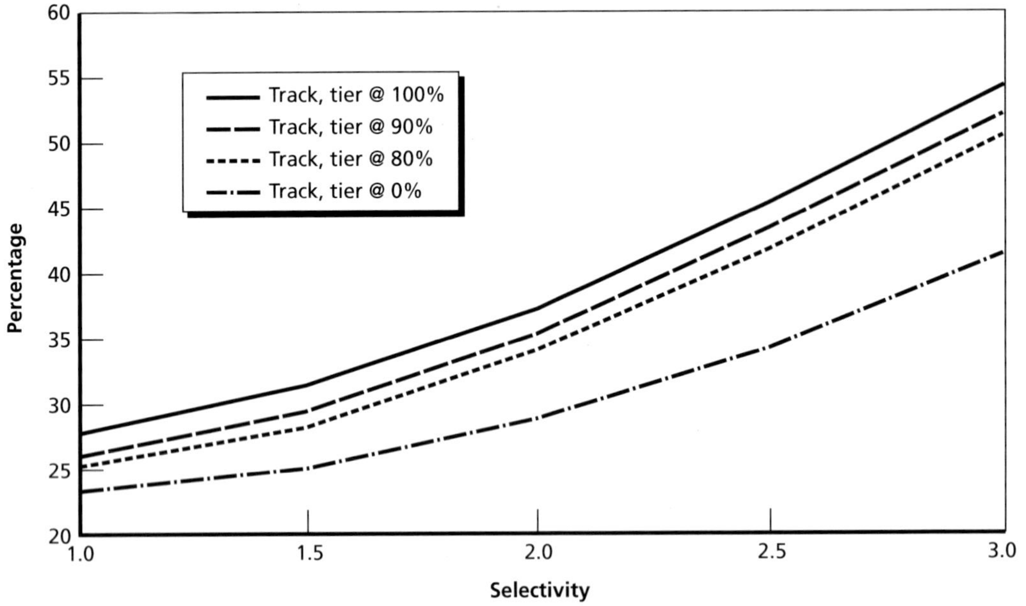

NOTE: In these cases, all GO inflows had to come from graduating fast-track colonels, and the occupational mix of such graduates needed only to meet, not exceed, the minimum GO inflow requirements.
RAND *TR759-3.1*

fully. Figure 3.2 shows how the same range of parameter settings affects the share of incoming colonels whose primary and paired skills both can be at least somewhat flexible. At the high end, up to 28 percent of the new colonels could have such occupational flexibility, and at the low end only about 7 percent.

After briefly summarizing differences between this and related RAND flow models, we describe in Chapter Four two solutions from this model where the policy limits were varied that govern selectivity for O-6 positions, how many more graduating colonels than new GOs should have each required a combination of primary and paired skills and how many of them must come from the fast track, and adherence to colonel positions' track and tier requirements.

Comparison with Previous GO and Career-Field Models

For any students of personnel flow modeling and force planning, it seems worth noting major similarities and differences among this and RAND's other recent and closely related modeling frameworks (refer to Table 3.3):

- The framework for senior executives first addressed the Air Force's GO and SES workforces and was the first in this family of models (Robbert et al., 2005). It addressed

Figure 3.2
How Parameter Settings Affect the Maximum Share of New Colonels with Some Flexibility in Both Primary and Paired Skills

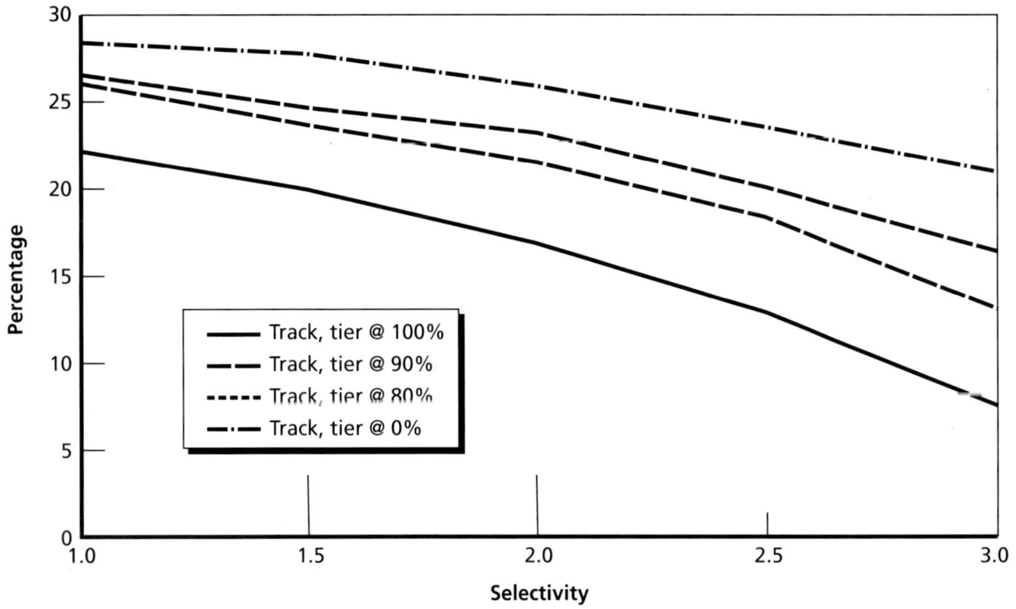

NOTE: In these cases, all GO inflows had to come from graduating fast-track colonels, and the occupational mix of such graduates needed only to meet, not exceed, the minimum GO inflow requirements.
RAND *TR759-3.2*

primary and paired skills.[14] Similar models were developed subsequently for the Army's and Navy's forces of military flag officers.[15]

- The model for Air Force space/missile officers was the first to reflect learning, i.e., the accumulation of backgrounds as officers progressed within and between grades (Vernez et al., 2006).
- The framework for Army unit commander development was the first to trace modeled officers' full work histories, maintaining detail about their assignment sequences, not merely their accumulation of experiences.[16]
- The model addressing GOs in the U.S. Air Force Reserve is unpublished, to date. It was the first to use a nonlinear mathematical formulation.[17]

---

[14] Paired skills were called "secondary" skills in that work.

[15] The work for the Army is unpublished. The Navy work is described in Lawrence M. Hanser, Louis W. Miller, Herbert J. Shukiar, and Bruce O. Newsome, *Developing Senior Navy Leaders: Requirements for Flag Officer Expertise Today and in the Future,* Santa Monica, Calif.: RAND Corporation, MG-618-NAVY, 2008.

[16] Henry A. Leonard, J. Michael Polich, Jeffrey D. Peterson, Ronald E. Sortor, and S. Craig Moore, *Something Old, Something New: Army Leader Development in a Dyanmic Environment,* Santa Monica, Calif.: RAND Corporation, MG-281-A, 2006.

[17] It occurred later than the work on active component colonels addressed in this report. In actuality, the nonlinear formulation eventually was optimized through the use of linear splines, enabling its conversion to a linear optimization.

Table 3.3
Similarities and Differences Among RAND's Recent Officer Flow Models

		Senior Executives	Space/Missile Operations Officers	Unit Commander Development	AFR GOs	O-6 Targets
Input data						
	Position requirements	x	x	x	x	x
	Loss rates		x	x		x
	Grade/stage durations	x	x	x		x
	Distribution targets				x	x
	Inflow total	x				
	Outflow targets			x		x
Scope						
	Military	x	x	x	x	x
	Civilian	x				
	Multiple specialties	x			x	x
	Grades	GO/SES	O-1 through O-6	O-1 through O-3	GO	O-6
	Stages within grades		x	x		x
	Nonoccupational backgrounds		x	x		
	Selectivity	x			x	x
Analytics						
	Steady state	x	x	x	x	x
	Flexible skills				x	x
	Tracks		x	x		x
	Qualifications grow		x	x		
	Full assignment history			x		
	Substitution across specialties	x			x	x
	Substitution across experience levels		x	x		x
	Substitution across tracks		x	x		x
	Retention variable	x		x	x	
	Sojourns variable				x	
	Linear	x	x	x		x
	GAMS	x	x	x	x	x
Outputs						
	Inflow total		x	x	x	x
	Mix of backgrounds in inflow	x			x	x
	Background growth		x	x		
	Retention and promotion	x		x	x	
	Assignments	x	x	x	x	x
	Grade/stage durations				x	

The model in this document, addressing the active component's O-6 force, was the first to include flexible occupational categories in its solutions and to let prior distributions influence its recommendations.

All of these models

- address position requirements stated in terms of specialty, grades, and occupational skills
- treat (at least) military officers
- model personnel systems in steady state
- use the GAMS programming language.[18]

But they differ in important respects, especially their scopes.

Several terms in Table 3.3 probably warrant somewhat more definition:

- Position requirements: These are the numbers of positions at each grade/stage needing each combination of backgrounds.[19]
- Grade/stage durations: These are the average sojourns in the various grades/stages.
- Distribution targets: These are the preferred mix of occupational backgrounds (a reference point).
- Outflow targets: These are the numbers or mix of skills to either be promoted or be candidates for promotion to higher grades.
- Nonoccupational backgrounds: This information defines specific operational, organizational, or leadership experiences, for example, those beyond one's technical specialization(s).
- Selectivity: This represents the number of qualified candidates available when vacancies occur.
- Flexible skills: Some personnel inventory categories include multiple occupational specialties (e.g., "rated" includes fighter pilots and bomber weapons officers, and "any acquisition" includes scientists, engineers, and acquisition managers).[20]
- Retention variable: The models recommend continuation or promotion rates rather than receiving them as input data.
- Sojourns variable: The lengths of time that individuals spend in grades or career stages are variable, not merely input data.
- Linear: The mathematical formulation includes the decision variables only in linear functional expressions.[21]
- Assignments: This information gives the alignments between positions and (modeled) personnel, that is, the categories of people who should fill the various categories of positions and how much of the time.

---

[18] Anthony Brooke, David Kendrick, and Alexander Meeraus, *GAMS, Release 2.25, A User's Guide,* Washington, D.C.: The Scientific Press, 1998.

[19] The Army version of the senior-executives model represented positions individually instead of in groups calling for the same primary and paired skills. The Navy version addressed only military flag officers (the admiralty) and did not allow (or need) substitutions across occupational specialties.

[20] These are *collector* categories or *bins* on the supply (people) side that match collections or bins of positions on the demand (or requirements) side.

[21] The Navy flag-officer model introduced a minimum threshold on promotions to ensure that its solutions were free of small numbers: If any members of an occupational pairing were to be promoted, then at least 0.3 must be promoted per year, that is, at least one about every three years. This made it a mixed-integer linear model.

CHAPTER FOUR

Two Optimal Solutions: The Basis for FY 2006's Occupational Development Floors

Solutions to the flow-optimization problem using different settings for several input parameters underlay the revised occupational developmental floors proposed for the Air Force's officer development teams. Table 4.1 delineates those parameter or policy settings. Each solution identified minimum annual colonel inflows, or floors, that would satisfy the specified policy limits, on average. The second set of policy settings was notably more demanding than the first (e.g., it targeted selectivity of at least three qualified candidates per O-6 opening rather than two, and at least 90 percent fulfillment of O-6 positions' requirements for appropriately experienced officers and for fast-track officers rather than 50 percent). Both solutions met fully the colonel positions' skill requirements and the minimum skill requirements for new GOs.

Both solutions defined floors; the preferred solution simply defined higher floors. The more new colonels with an occupational pair, the more likely there will be enough qualified candidates when such openings occur. Further, the more properly experienced colonels with an occupational pair, the more likely there will be enough candidates when corresponding openings occur. And so on. For example:

- The marginal solution demonstrated that 87.3 (72 percent) of the 121 O-6 jobs that were open to RT (any rated) skill and that needed no paired skill could be filled using a flexible inventory of 11Y (pilots) with no paired skill (None). But the preferred solution found

Table 4.1
Parameter Settings Yielding Marginal and Preferred Selectivity, Position Matches, and Flows

Control Parameter	*Marginal*: For Floors Yielding Lower Selectivity and Poorer Person-Job Matches	*Preferred*: For Floors Yielding Higher Selectivity and Better Person-Job Matches
Selectivity for each position must be at least	2	3
Minimum percentage of positions that must be filled by colonels at the designated experience level	50	90
Minimum percentage of fast-track positions that must be filled by fast-track colonels	50	90
Minimum percentage of O-7 inflow that must be filled by fast-track colonels	90	100
Multiplier for minimum O-7 inflow requirement	1	2

that only 49.9 (41 percent) still had that much flexibility, and instead used more specific primary skills—e.g., 6.5 (5 percent) 11Fs (fighter pilots), 7.7 (6 percent) 11Rs (reconnaissance pilots), and 2.9 (2 percent) 11Hs (helicopter pilots)—and with paired skills—e.g., 9.6 (7.9 percent) with 16P (political-military), 2.3 (2 percent) with 14N (intelligence), 9.1 (8 percent) with APE (aerospace power employment), and 5.2 (4 percent) with 2YY/63A (either logistics or acquisition management).
- The marginal solution found that 71.6 (82 percent) of the 87 O-6 jobs that were open to 6YY (any acquisition/finance primary skill) and did not need a paired skill could be filled using officers without paired skills. But the preferred solution used only 36.3 (42 percent) without paired skills, instead recommending, for example, 7.2 (8 percent) with paired skill 63A (acquisition management), 10 (12 percent) with MO (mobility operations), and 14.8 (17 percent) with 13SYC/21M (either missiles or munitions/missile maintenance).

Let us first consider the average annual cohorts of new colonels that the optimizations recommended and then the alignments between positions and colonels (i.e., the optimization's assignments of categories of modeled officers to categories of jobs) at the various levels of experience.

Average Annual Cohorts of New Colonels

Appendix D tabulates the inflow portions of the two solutions, for example, recommending in the preferred case (compared with the marginal case)

- about twice as many per year in the flexible category that includes 1YF (fighter pilots and navigators), with twice as many in that group bringing each of six paired skills, by far the most common being APE (aerospace power employment) and 16P (international political-military affairs)
- about 20 percent more new 13SYC (missile) colonels per year in total, including roughly twice as many with a paired skill in 16R (plans and programs), twice as many with Acq (acquisition), 75 percent more with 21MYA (munitions and missile maintenance), and none without a paired skill
- about the same number of new 14N (intelligence) colonels per year (only 4 percent fewer), but about 90 percent more with a paired skill in 16R (plans and programs), 75 percent more in IO (information operations), 70 percent more in APE (aerospace power employment), and none without a paired skill
- about one-third more new colonels per year in 21B (equipment maintenance), the majority still needing no paired skill, but roughly twice as many with each of five paired skills: 63A (acquisition management), E&T (education and training), 21M (munitions and missile maintenance), 32E (civil engineering), and 13S (space or missile operations)
- about two-thirds more colonels per year in 31P (security forces) and one-third more in 32E (civil engineering), the lion's shares still not needing paired skills
- about 60 percent fewer new 36P (personnel) colonels per year, although about twice as many with paired skills in 33Y (communications and information systems) and in 61S (scientists), and none without a paired skill

- about 50 percent more new 64P (contracting) colonels per year, including nearly twice as many with paired skills in 13SYE (space warning) and in 36P (personnel)
- about 70 percent more new colonels per year in 65F (financial management), still nearly 80 percent of them not needing a paired skill.

Table 4.2 lists several summary characteristics of those inflows. Because the preferred solution recommended a higher percentage of new colonels on the fast track, where anticipated service as colonels is somewhat longer, its entry cohort would be somewhat (about 2 percent) smaller. The analysis recommended that at least 31 percent of the new colonels have paired skills (according to the marginal solution), but preferably at least 58 percent of them (nearly twice the share, according to the preferred solution). This compares with our observation in Chapter Two that only about 22 percent of the colonel positions, in total, called for paired skills. About the same share (88 percent) of new fast-track colonels needed paired skills in both the marginal and preferred solutions. But the share of other new colonels (those not necessarily on the fast track) needing paired skills more than doubled in the preferred solution, rising to 42 percent from 18 percent. Occupational flexibility also decreased (e.g., 26 percent of the marginal solution's incoming cohort had some flexibility in both its primary and paired skills, compared with the preferred solution's 8 percent). In spite of such differences, nearly two-thirds of the entry cohort was the same in both solutions.[1]

Before reviewing the skill pairings recommended for each broad occupational category, we must address several small elements of the targeted O-6 entry cohort that optimization found it unnecessary to commit to a single occupational category:

Table 4.2
Summary Measures for Recommended Cohorts of New Colonels

Averages	Marginal	Preferred
Entrants per year	458	449
Percentage of entrants on fast track	18	35
Percentage of entrants with paired skills		
Fast track	88	88
Not fast track	18	42
Total	31	58
Occupational flexibility		
Percentage with a primary skill	39	32
Percentage with a paired skill	77	57
Percentage with both	26	8
Pecentage with neither	10	19

[1] For example, the marginal solution recommended an average 10.2 new fighter (1YF) colonels per year, with six different paired skills (mostly aerospace power employment). The preferred solution recommended roughly twice as many new 1YFs with each paired skill, so the two solutions had 10.2 generic fighter specialists in common.

- The model recommended a new colonel every few years with primary skill 11B/12B/13SYC (bombers or missiles) and paired skill 14N (intelligence). We consigned that flow to 11B/12B (bombers), within the rated category, because 13SYC (missile) was already further above its previous share of colonels than was the bomber skill.
- The model recommended about one to three new colonels per year from 1YR/14N (reconnaissance or intelligence), with paired skill 63A (acquisition management). We charged 14N (intelligence), within the nonrated operations category, with that flow because it was below and 1YR (reconnaissance) was above its previous share of colonels.
- The marginal solution included a new colonel rarely (about every five years) from either 14N (intelligence) or 33S (communications and information systems). Because it was less burdened with paired skills than 14N and because its only other link with intelligence was via IO (information operations), we tagged 33S with providing that colonel, also requiring a paired skill in intelligence.
- The model recommended about one to three new colonels per year from either Acq (acquisition) or 2YY (logistics), with paired skill 86M (operations management) or 86P (command and control). We gave 21X (logistics) responsibility for providing those colonels because acquisition was charged with producing a larger share of colonels with other paired skills.

With those few cross-category flexibilities resolved, we can next review the skill pairings recommended for each broad occupational category. We will see recommendations that relatively more new nonrated operations colonels and relatively fewer new support colonels bring paired skills, compared with new rated, logistics, and acquisition/finance colonels.[2]

Paired Skills Recommended for Rated Colonels

The flow analysis anticipated about 150 to 190 new rated O-6s per year,[3] with at least 45 to 80 of them with paired skills. Table 4.3 summarizes the mixes of 19 paired skills recommended for ten groups of new rated colonels.[4] First, the right-hand column recommended that at least 24 percent of all new rated colonels have paired skills (the marginal solution's percentage) and preferably at least 53 percent (the preferred solution's percentage). The most common paired

---

[2] Several categories of primary occupations are merged in this discussion, with the aim of simplifying the floors that development teams consider. Appendix D makes clear that the model and the position requirements make the following distinctions that these consolidations mask: (1) pilot versus either pilot or navigator for some weapon systems, such as 11B (bomber pilot) versus 11B/12B (bomber, including both pilots and navigators); (2) categories of pilot (e.g., fighter versus experimental/test versus astronaut); (3) airlift versus tanker for mobility; (4) shreds and combinations thereof for "space" (e.g., 13SYA [satellite C2] versus 13SYD/E [space surveillance or warning]); and (5) other previous career fields that merged into 21R (logistics readiness): 21G (logistics plans), 21S (supply), and 21T (transportation).

[3] The range stems from the two solutions' different allocations of flexible positions to the rated occupations. Ranges for all occupational categories have the same source: how the two solutions allocated the flexible positions.

[4] Recall that the optimization did not peg inflows to specific occupations unnecessarily. In the preferred solution, for example, 30 percent of the annual rated O-6 inflow was in categories that cut across Air Force development teams (e.g., "fighter, bomber, or mobility," "mobility or SOF," and "astronaut"). The marginal solution's corresponding figure was 53 percent. To calculate percentage floors separately for each rated development team, relative to its total inflow, such flexible inflows must be allocated to specific rated categories and corresponding development teams. This should be done carefully because the shares of officers with secondary occupations (versus without) differ from one flexible occupational group to another. Chapter Five notes different allocation approaches and describes the one used in 2005 to convert model recommendations into specific floors for the development teams.

Table 4.3
Minimum Percentages of New Rated Colonels with Paired Skills

			Primary Skill										
			CAF					MAF	SOF		Shared		
Paired Skill			Fighter and Bomber Combined	Fighter	Bomber	Reconnaissance and ABM Combined	Reconnaissance	Mobility	Helicopter and SOF Combined	SOF	Pilot	Rated, Not ABM	All Rated Combined
Marginal Solution (Lower Selectivity and Poorer Person-Job Matches)													
1	APE	Aerospace power employment	5.1	4.5	.6	.2		.9	.8	.8	.7	6.9	7.1
2	MO	Mobility operations						.7				.7	.7
3	IO	Information operations	.2		.2	.1						.2	.7
4	EW	Electronic warfare											.7
5	13SYA/ B/D/E	Any space	.0		.0	.0						.0	.0
6	14N	Intelligence	.1		.1							.1	1.2
7	16P	International political-military affairs	1.4	1.1	.4	.0		.1	.0	.0		1.6	1.6
8	16R	Plans/programs	1.1	1.0	.1			1.0	.9	.6	.8	3.0	3.7
9	2YY/ 63A	Any logistics or acquisition management									.7	.7	.7
10	21R	Logistics readiness	.2		.2				.2	.2		.4	.4
11	36P/ 38M	Personnel or manpower							.3	.3	.4	.7	.7
12	E&T	Education and training	.2	.2								.2	.2
13	6YY	Acquisiiton/financial management	.6		.6				.7	.7	.6	1.4	1.4
14	Acq	Any acquisition	1.1	1.1		.3	.3				1.1	1.4	1.4
15	62E/ 63A	Developmental engineering or acquisition management										.7	.7
16	62EYF	Flight test developmental engineering									.6	.6	.6
17	63A	Acquisiiton management	.4	.2	.3			.8				1.6	1.6
18	RQ	Requirements	.1		.1	.0						.1	.1
19	T&E	Test and evaluation	.1	.1	.1							.1	.1
20	None	None	12.8	9.5	.6	3.7	.7	10.7	2.0	.5	68.5	73.4	76.3
Minimum with paired skill			10.8	8.1	2.7	.7	.3	3.6	2.9	2.7	5.1	20.6	23.7

Table 4.3—Continued

			Primary Skill										
			CAF					MAF	SOF		Shared		
Paired Skill			Fighter and Bomber Combined	Fighter	Bomber	Reconnaissance and ABM Combined	Reconnaissance	Mobility	Helicipter and SOF Combined	SOF	Pilot	Rated, Not ABM	All Rated Combined
Preferred Solution (Higher Selectivity and Better Person-Job Matches)													
1	APE	Aerospace power employment	12.7	11.3	1.5	.4		2.2	2.0	2.0	1.7	17.1	17.5
2	MO	Mobility operations						1.8				1.8	1.8
3	IO	Information operations	.6		.1	.3						.6	1.8
4	EW	Electronic warfare											1.8
5	13SYA/ B/D/E	Any space	.0		.0	.1						.0	.1
6	14N	Intelligence	.3		.3							.3	1.9
7	16P	International political-military affairs	3.5	2.6	.9	.1		.3	.1	.1		4.0	4.0
8	16R	Plans/programs	2.7	2.4	.3			2.8	1.7	1.5	2.0	7.2	7.2
9	2YY/ 63A	Any logistics or acquisition management									1.8	1.8	1.8
10	21R	Logistics readiness	.4		.4				.5	.5		1.0	1.0
11	36P/ 38M	Personnel or manpower							.6	.6	1.0	1.7	1.7
12	E&T	Education and training	.4	.4								.4	.4
13	6YY	Acquisition/financial management	1.6		1.6				1.8	1.8	1.6	3.4	3.4
14	Acq	Any acquisition	1.7	1.7		.6	.6	.5			1.7	2.8	2.8
15	62E/ 63A	Developmental engineering or acquisition management											
16	62EYF	Flight test developmental engineering									1.5	1.5	1.5
17	63A	Acquisition management	1.1	.4	.7			1.5				3.3	3.3
18	RQ	Requirements	.2		.2	.0						.2	.2
19	T&E	Test and evaluation	.4	.2	.2							.4	.4
20	None	None							.6	.6	1.0	1.7	1.7
Minimum with paired skill			25.6	18.9	6.2	1.5	.6	9.2	6.7	6.6	11.3	47.4	52.6

NOTE: All percentages represent shares of average total new rated colonels per year (about 187 marginal, about 151 preferred).

skills should be APE (aerospace power employment) and 16R (plans/programs), although the different varieties of acquisition experience (including lines 14–19 in each part of the table) totaled more than plans/programs. 16P (international political-military affairs) was also prominent. To help interpret the table, here are a few examples of more specific recommendations from the bottom half (representing the preferred solution):

- An average of at least 1.8 percent of new rated O-6s should have IO (information operations) as a paired skill, including at least 0.6 percent fighter or bomber officers (as long as at least 0.1 percent are bomber officers) and at least 0.3 percent reconnaissance officers or air battle managers.[5] The other 0.9 percent can have these or other aeronautical ratings.[6]
- At least 1.8 percent should have EW (electronic warfare) as a paired skill, and it does not matter which aeronautical rating they have.
- At least 1.9 percent should have 14N (intelligence) as a paired skill, including at least 0.3 percent (about one out of six of that minimum) bomber officers. The remainder can have any aeronautical rating.
- At least 0.4 percent should have a fighter rating, with E&T (education and training) as a paired skill.

There was room for many new rated colonels without paired skills although less room than the position requirements alone implied. According to the experts, up to 78 percent of the rated positions could be filled by officers lacking paired skills. But flow analysis recommended allowing no more than 76 percent and preferably no more than 47 percent of new rated colonels without paired skills.

Paired Skills Recommended for Nonrated Operations Colonels

Flow analysis recommended an average of roughly 45 to 60 new colonels per year with nonrated operations primary skills, about 20 to 25 of them from space and missile operations (13S), about 21 to 22 from 14N (intelligence), about one to three each from 13D (control and recovery) and 13M (airfield operations), and about three to four from 15W (weather). Table 4.4 shows that most new colonels from nonrated operations career fields needed paired skills, preferably at least 93 percent, but with a lower limit of 62 percent, even though only about 48 percent of the positions requiring nonrated operations officers called for paired skills. Among the nonrated operations career fields, only 13D colonels did not need paired skills, although they could become candidates for more O-6 positions if they had paired skills. All 13M colonels should have communications and information systems as their paired skill. Ideally, all new

---

[5] Note that the right-hand column in Table 4.3 is not the simple sum of the percentages in the table's other columns, because some of the columns have overlapping scopes. For example, the column "Fighter and Bomber Combined" includes percentages for the separate "Fighter" and "Bomber" columns: (a) In total, at least 0.6 percent of new rated colonels should have primary experience in fighters or bombers and paired skill in IO, and (b) at least 0.1 percent of new rated colonels should have primary experience in bombers and paired skill in IO. Even the "Bomber" column already represents two primary groups in Appendix D: 11B (bomber pilot) and 11B/12B (bomber).

[6] Recall that the optimization's numbers represent averages. Because the preferred solution recommended averaging about 151 new rated colonels per year, 1.8 percent of them with the IO paired skill amounts to 2.7 per year or at least eight every three years, 0.6 percent out of those 1.8 percent coming from fighters or bombers amounts to least four every five years, 0.1 percent from bombers amounts to at least one every six years, 0.3 percent from reconnaissance or air battle management amounts to at least one every other year, and 0.9 percent from any aeronautical rating amounts to at least six every five years.

Table 4.4
Minimum Percentages of New Colonels from Nonrated Operations with Paired Skills

			Primary Skill							
			13D	13M	13S			14N	15W	
Paired Skill			Control and Recovery	Airfield Operations	Space or Missile	Any Space	Missile	Intelligence	Weather	Nonrated Operations Total
Marginal Solution (Lower Selectivity and Poorer Person-Job Matches)										
1	APE	Aerospace power employment			7	6		9		7
2	IO	Information operations			3	1		12		7
3	13S	Space or missile						6		3
4	13SYC	Missile			8	8				3
5	14N	Intelligence			.2	.2				.1
6	16F	Foreign area						7		3
7	16P	International political-military affairs			6		1	.1		3
8	16R	Plans/programs			8	3	1	7	38	10
9	21MYA	Munitions and missile maintenance, missile			10		10			4
10	33Y	Communications		100	1	1		2		4
11	36P/38M	Personnel or manpower						1		1
12	E&T	Education and training			6			6		5
13	Acq	Any acquisition			26	20	6			11
14	63A	Acquisiiton management			3	3				1
15	RQ	Requirements			1	1				.5
Minimum with paired skill			0	100	79	44	18	50	38	62
Preferred Solution (Higher Selectivity and Better Person-Job Matches)										
1	APE	Aerospace power employment			9	8		16		10
2	IO	Information operations			3	1		22		9
3	13S	Space or missile						13		4
4	13SYC	Missile			10	10				5
5	14N	Intelligence			.3	.3				.1
6	16F	Foreign area						14		5
7	16P	International political-military affairs			8		1	.2		4
8	16R	Plans/programs			10	4	1	14	69	15
9	21MYA	Munitions and missile maintenance, missile			12		12			6
10	33Y	Communications		100	2	2		4		6
11	36P/38M	Personnel or manpower						3		1
12	E&T	Education and training			8			13		8
13	Acq	Any acquisition			34	26	8			18
14	63A	Acquisition management			3	3				2
15	RQ	Requirements			1	1				1
Minimum with paired skill			0	100	100	57	22	100	69	93

NOTE: All percentages represent shares of average total new nonrated operations colonels per year (about 47 marginal, about 612 preferred).

13S[7] and 14N colonels also would bring paired skills, but lower limits for their average shares with paired skills were 79 percent and 50 percent, respectively. The percentages in Table 4.4's columns for 13S refer to the total number of new 13S colonels per year, including both space and missile officers. For example, according to the preferred solution, (a) 10 percent of the new 13S colonels should have a paired skill in 13SYC (missiles), and, naturally, only space officers (not missileers) needed that paired skill, (b) 12 percent of the new 13S colonels should have a paired skill in 21MYA (missile maintenance) and all should be missileers, and (c) 8 percent of new 13S colonels should have a paired skill in E&T (education and training) and they could be from any 13S shredout. The total row indicates that more new space colonels than missile colonels needed secondary occupations: 57 percent out of 100 percent in the preferred solution and 44 percent out of 79 percent in the marginal solution.[8] Finally, preferably, at least 69 percent of 15W colonels would bring paired skill in 16R (plans/programs).

Paired Skills Recommended for Logistics Colonels

The flow analyses favored about 54 to 64 new logistics colonels per year, with about 30 to 45 from maintenance and about 15 to 18 from logistics readiness. At least 20 to 35 of them should bring paired skills, the closer to 35 (or above 35) the better. Table 4.5 indicates that at least 37 percent of new logistics colonels should bring paired skills, but preferably at least 56 percent, even though only about 11 percent of the logistics positions apparently needed colonels with paired skills. 63A (acquisition management) was the largest paired skill recommended for logisticians, but a significant share needed a paired skill in another area of logistics. For example, at least 3 to 5 percent of the total should come from logistics plans and have a paired skill in maintenance, supply, or transportation.[9] Another 2 to 3 percent should come from logistics readiness and have secondary competency in maintenance, and still another 2 to 4 percent should come from logistics readiness and have secondary competency in either acquisition (but not necessarily acquisition management) or (equipment) maintenance.

Paired Skills Recommended for New Colonels from Support and OSI

The flow analyses recommended about 85 to 90 new support and Office of Special Investigations (OSI) colonels per year, with at least 18 to 32 of them having paired skills. 33S (communications and information systems), 32E (civil engineering), and personnel and manpower

---

7 Note that Table 4.4's column labeled "any space" combines several more detailed 13S shredouts: 13SYA (space satellite C2), 13SYB (space lift), 13SYD (space surveillance), 13SYE (space warning), and all flexible combinations thereof—for example, 13SYA/D/E (space satellite C2, surveillance, or warning).

8 The latter does not imply that new space colonels must outnumber new missile colonels. For example, it would be acceptable to bring in 44 percent with primarily space background and a paired skill, another 35 percent with primarily missile background and a paired skill (to bring to 79 percent the total number with a paired skill), and the other 21 percent with either space or missile primary background and no paired skill. It would be easier to manage the O-6 and GO forces, however, if at least 57 percent of the new 13S colonels were space specialists with paired skills, at least 22 percent were missile specialists with paired skills, and the other 21 percent also had paired skills.

9 When logistics experts identified the positions' requirements in 2002, the career field was in flux, shifting to a new classification structure. Some requirements were stated in terms of the new structure and some in terms of the old. Table 4.5 presents O-6 inflow floors derived from the information in that mixed form. We noted that the 21X development team might use only Table 4.5's columns labeled "all maintenance combined," "all log readiness," and "Logistics total." In that case, the logistics secondary occupation for logistics readiness officers would be maintenance, and at least 5 to 8 percent of new logistics colonels should bring that combination.

Table 4.5
Minimum Percentages of New Logistics Colonels with Paired Skills

			Primary Skill							
			Shared	Maintenance				Logistics Readiness		
Paired Skill			Equipment Maintenance or Log Readiness	All Maintenance Combined	Equipment Maintenance	Munitions and Missile Maintenance	Munitions and Missile Maintenance, Spacelift	All Log Readiness Combined	Logistics Plans	Logistics Total
Marginal Solution (Lower Selectivity and Poorer Person-Job Matches)										
1	86M/86P	Operations management or C2								2
2	13S	Space or missile	2	2	2					2
3	16P	International political-military affairs	.3					.3		.3
4	16R	Plans/programs	.4					.4		2
5	2YY	Any logistics	3					3	3	3
6	21A/B/M	Maintenance	2					2		2
7	21M	Munitions and missile maintenance	2	2	2					2
8	21R	Logistics readiness		1						1
9	32E	Civil engineering	2	2	2					2
10	33Y	Communications		3		3	3			3
11	Acq/21M	Any acquisition or equipment maintenance	2					2	2	2
12	63A	Acquisition management	7	6	3	3		.4		10
13	64P	Contracting		1						1
14	65F	Financial management	.4					.4		.4
15	E&T	Education and training	2	2	2					2
Minimum with paired skill			24	20	12	6	3	8	5	37
Preferred Solution (Higher Selectivity and Better Person-Job Matches)										
1	86M/86P	Operations management or C2								4
2	13S	Space or missile	4	4	4					4
3	16P	International political-military affairs	.5					.5		.5
4	16R	Plans/programs	4					4		4
5	2YY	Any logistics	5					5	5	5
6	21A/B/M	Maintenance	3					3		3
7	21M	Munitions and missile maintenance	4	4	4					4
8	21R	Logistics readiness		2						2
9	32E	Civil engineering	4	4	4					4
10	33Y	Communications		5		5	5			5
11	Acq/21M	Any acquisition or equipment maintenance	4					4	4	4
12	63A	Acquisition management	5	10	5	5		1		10
13	64P	Contracting		2						2
14	65F	Financial management	1					1		1
15	E&T	Education and training	4	4	4					4
Minimum with paired skill			38	34	21	10	5	17	9	56

NOTE: All percentages represent shares of average total new logistics colonels per year (about 54 marginal, about 64 preferred).

(then 36P and 38M) were the largest support career fields. Table 4.6 indicates that relatively fewer new support and OSI colonels needed paired skills: preferably at least 36 percent, but, less beneficially, as few as 21 percent. In comparison, only about 7 percent of the positions requiring support and OSI colonels apparently needed officers with paired skills. The most common paired skills for this group were plans/programs and political-military affairs. For purposes of matching identified requirements for paired skills, two of these career fields needed just one paired skill: at least 7 to 10 percent of new 32E (civil engineering) colonels needed paired skill in 16R (plans/programs), and at least 11 percent of 71S (special investigations) needed the 31P (security forces) paired skill. At least 17 to 21 percent of new 31P (security forces) colonels needed paired skills in 21T/34M/E&T (either transportation, services, or education and training). New 34M (services) and 35B (band) colonels did not need paired skills. At least 19 to 34 percent of new 33S (communications and information system) colonels needed paired skills, mainly in IO (information operations), but also in 16P (political-military affairs) and 36P (personnel). For new 35P (public affairs) colonels, at least 42 to 51 percent should have paired skill in 16P (political-military affairs) and 28 to 35 percent in 16R (plans/programs). And at least 29 to 86 percent of (37F) manpower and personnel colonels should have paired skills, the largest shares in (33Y) communications and information systems, 13S (space or missile operations), 16R (plans/programs), and 61S (scientist).[10]

Paired Skills Recommended for New Colonels from Acquisition and Finance

The flow analyses favored about 80 to 85 new acquisition/finance colonels per year, at least 30 to 55 of them bringing paired skills. It is important to note that, paralleling the situation in the rated career fields, the flow model did not peg inflows to specific career fields unnecessarily. In these two solutions, from 12 to 22 percent of the annual O-6 inflow could come from multiple career fields—for example, some from either 62E (developmental engineering) or 63A (acquisition management), some from any acquisition career field (61S, 62E, 63A, or 64P), and others from either acquisition or finance (61S, 62E, 63A, 64P, or 65F). To calculate percentage floors separately for each of these development teams, relative to its total inflow, the flexible inflows would need to be allocated to specific teams (see Chapter Five).

Table 4.7 shows that, collectively, the acquisition and finance career fields needed about the same degree of skill pairing as the nonrated operations career fields. At least 36 to 68 percent of the new colonels needed a paired skill, and the closer to (or above) 68 percent the better, even though only about 29 percent of the acquisition and finance positions needed colonels with paired skills. As in some earlier tables, the numbers in the last column's cells are not necessarily sums of the other columns' numbers. Consider the 13SYE (space warning) row, for example, which says that at least 1.5 to 2.8 percent of the new acquisition/finance colonels should come from the contracting career field and have paired skill in space warning. In contrast, the 13SYD (space surveillance) row says that at least 1.4 to 2.8 percent should have space surveillance as a paired skill and that it does not matter from which acquisition/finance career field they come. More than half of the acquisition/finance group's minimum paired skills were in operations, nearly a third in space or missiles. Another quarter of the minimums were in

[10] By 2005, the previous 36P (personnel) and 38M (manpower) career fields had merged into 37F, whose development team we suggested could use only the column labeled "pers and mpwr combined," ignoring the distinctions between manpower and personnel that were explicit in 2002's position requirements and our flow analyses. Since then, they have merged further with 34M (services) into 38F (force support).

Table 4.6
Minimum Percentages of New Support and OSI Colonels with Paired Skills

			Primary Skill										
			31P	32E	33S	34M	35P		37F			71S	
Paired Skill			Security Forces	Civil Engineering	Communications and Information Systems	Services	Band	Public Affairs	Pers and Mpwr Combined	Personnel	Manpower	Special Investigations	Support and Osi Total
Marginal Solution (Lower Selectivity and Poorer Person-Job Matches)													
1	APE	Aerospace power employment							2				.5
2	IO	Information operations			10								3
3	13S	Space or missile							6	6			2
4	13SYA/B/D/E	Any space			.05								.02
5	14N	Intelligence			1								.3
6	16P	International political-military affairs			4			42	1				4
7	16R	Plans/programs		7				28	5				4
8	21T/34M/E&T	Transportation, services, or education and training	17										1
9	31P	Security forces										11	1
10	33Y	Communications and information systems							6	6			2
11	36P	Personnel			4				2		2		2
12	81T	Education and training							2				1
13	61S	Scientist							5	5			1
Minimum with paired skill			17	7	19	0	0	71	29	16	2	11	21
Preferred Solution (Higher Selectivity and Better Person-Job Matches)													
1	APE	Aerospace power employment							5				1
2	IO	Information operations			11								3
3	13S	Space or missile							17	17			3
4	13SYA/B/D/E	Any space			.15								.04
5	14N	Intelligence											
6	16P	International political-military affairs			12			51	2				7
7	16R	Plans/programs		10				35	15				7
8	21T/34M/E&T	Transportation, services, or education and training	21										3
9	31P	Security forces										11	1
10	33Y	Communications and information systems							17	17			3
11	36P	Personnel			11				7		7		4
12	81T	Education and training							7				1
13	61S	Scientist							15	15			3
Minimum with paired skill			21	10	34	0	0	86	86	49	7	11	36

Table 4.7
Minimum Percentages of New Colonels from Acquisition and Finance with Paired Skills

			Primary Skill								
			Shared		61S		62E	63A	64P	65F	
Paired Skill			Any Acquisition	Scientist or Developmental Engineering	Scientist	Analytical Scientist	Developmental Engineering	Acquisition Management	Contracting	Financial Management	Acquisition/Finance Total
Marginal Solution (Lower Selectivity and Poorer Person-Job Matches)											
1	APE	Aerospace power employment	.1					.1			.1
2	IO	Information operations	1.9	1.6	1.6			.3			1.9
3	MO	Mobility operations									1.6
4	13B/D/M	C2ISR	1.0					1.0			1.0
5	13B	Air battle manager	.7					.7			.7
6	13S	Space or missile	1.4	1.4	1.4	1.4					1.4
7	13S/14N	Space, missile, or intelligence	.7	.7			.7				.7
8	13SYA	Space satellite C2	2.9								2.9
9	13SYA/B/D/E	Any space	.3					.3			.3
10	13SYB	Space lift	2.8								2.8
11	13SYB/C	Space lift or missile	.6	.6			.6				.6
12	13SYC/21M	Missile or munitions and missile maintenance									1.5
13	13SYD	Space surveillance	1.4								1.4
14	13SYE	Space warning	1.5						1.5		1.5
15	SA	Safety								.1	.1
16	16P/16R	Plans/programs or international political-military affairs	1.9					1.9			1.9
17	16R	Plans/programs								.5	.5
18	16R/21R/33Y	Plans/programs, logistics readiness, or communications								.2	.2
19	21A/B/M	Maintenance	.2					.2			.2
20	21R	Logistics readiness	.2					.2			.2
21	2YY	Any logistics	1.5					1.5			1.5
22	33Y	Communications	.5					.5			.5
23	36P	Personnel	2.3	1.4	1.4				.8		2.3
24	Acq	Any acquisition	1.6	1.4			1.4	.1		1.4	3.0
25	61S/62E	Scientist or developmental enginering	1.0					1.0			1.0
26	62E	Developmental engineering	1.6					1.6			1.6
27	63A	Acquisition management	3.5	3.5	1.8						3.5
28	64P	Contracting	.1					.1			.1
29	65F	Financial management	.5					.5			.5
Minimum with paired skill			30.1	10.7	6.3	1.4	2.8	10.0	2.3	2.3	35.5

Table 4.7—Continued

			Primary Skill								
			Shared		61S		62E	63A	64P	65F	
Paired Skill			Any Acquisition	Scientist or Developmental Engineering	Scientist	Analytical Scientist	Developmental Engineering	Acquisition Management	Contracting	Financial Management	Acquisition/Finance Total
		Preferred Solution (Higher Selectivity and Better Person-Job Matches)									
1	APE	Aerospace power employment	.3					.3			.3
2	IO	Information operations	3.8	3.3	3.3			.5			3.8
3	MO	Mobility operations									3.3
4	13B/D/M	C2ISR	2.1					2.1			2.1
5	13B	Air battle manager	1.2					1.2			1.2
6	13S	Space or missile	2.8	2.8	2.8	2.8					2.8
7	13S/14N	Space, missile, or intelligence	.2	.2			.2				.2
8	13SYA	Space satellite C2	5.2								5.2
9	13SYA/B/D/E	Any space	.5					.5			.5
10	13SYB	Space lift	5.2								5.2
11	13SYB/C	Space lift or missile	1.0	1.0			1.0				1.0
12	13SYC/21M	Missile or munitions and missile maintenance									2.9
13	13SYD	Space surveillance	2.8								2.8
14	13SYE	Space warning	2.8						2.8		2.8
15	SA	Safety								.3	.3
16	16P/16R	Plans/programs or international political-military affairs	3.9					3.9			3.9
17	16R	Plans/programs								.6	.6
18	16R/21R/33Y	Plans/programs, logistics readiness, or communications								.8	.8
19	21A/B/M	Maintenance	.5					.5			.5
20	21R	Logistics readiness	.3					.3			.3
21	2YY	Any logistics	3.0					3.0			3.0
22	33Y	Communications	1.0					1.0			1.0
23	36P	Personnel	4.5	2.8	2.8				1.6		4.5
24	Acq	Any acquisition	2.8	2.8			2.8			2.8	5.7
25	61S/62E	Scientist or developmental enginering	1.6					1.6			1.6
26	62E	Developmental engineering	3.2					3.2			3.2
27	63A	Acquisition management	7.0	7.0	4.7						7.0
28	64P	Contracting	.1					.1			.1
29	65F	Financial management	.5					.5			.5
Minimum with paired skill			56.7	20.0	13.6	2.8	4.1	19.0	4.5	4.6	67.5

NOTE: All percentages represent shares of average total new acquisition/finance colonels per year (about 82 in both the marginal and preferred solutions).

other areas of acquisition/finance itself. For example, at least 1.6 to 3.2 percent of the new acquisition/finance colonels should come from 63A (acquisition management) and have paired skill in 62E (developmental engineering).

Alignments Between (Modeled) Colonels and Positions

The key to this analysis is that the optimization exploited the flexibility in the positions' requirements for track, experience level, and occupational skills in finding preferred mixes of colonels and ways of aligning them with appropriate positions.[11] *Optimal solutions did not fair-share the flexible positions.*[12] Table 4.8 summarizes how the two solutions recommended meeting positions' needs for experience and track. Consider the flexible requirements. For example, (1) the marginal solution recommended that fast-track colonels fill an average 3 percent + 2 percent + 6 percent = 11 percent of the positions that did not require them (i.e., that were flexibly open to either fast-track or not-fast-track colonels), while the preferred solution recommended 5 percent + 7 percent + 12 percent = 24 percent, and (2) the marginal solution recommended that colonels from the second experience level fill 2 percent + 18 percent = 19 percent of the positions

---

[11] We use the vaguer term *align* rather than *assign* here for two reasons: (1) Instead of distinct, individual officers assigned to specific jobs, our solutions represent categories of inventory, categories of jobs, and the average numbers of officers from each inventory category who could or should be assigned to each job category. In reality, actual assignments at any moment have integer values—for example, 10 colonels with Skill X are assigned to jobs that require Skill Y. But the alignments in our solutions seldom have integer values—for example, an average of 10.2 colonels with Skill X should be assigned to jobs that require Skill Y. (Sometimes the actual number assigned may be 8, 9, 10, 11, 12, or 13, say, but the average should hover around 10.2, in this notional example.) (2) The solutions allocate flexible jobs among eligible categories of inventory just as much as vice versa. At its core, the model exploits the jobs' flexibilities to accommodate and size sustainable experience pyramids for each inventory category.

[12] Fair-sharing allocates flexible positions in predetermined ratios among the categories of eligible colonels, ratios based on the numbers of other positions that call for those categories. For example, if 20 jobs called for Skill A, 30 for Skill B, and 25 for either A or B, fair-sharing would allocate 10 of the latter to Skill A and the other 15 to Skill B. Although it may seem reasonable and even equitable at first glance, AFPC analysts tried fair-sharing the requirements described in Chapter Two, using the primary and paired skill requirements while ignoring the track and experience requirements. The resulting skill-pairing targets (not documented) were very different from those that emerged later through this report's flow analysis. Among the 99 targets that fair-sharing yielded for 20 development teams:

- Only ten were consistent with (i.e., fell between) the marginal and preferred lower limits identified through flow analysis—for example, fair-sharing estimated that 7 percent of CAF officers needed the 16P (political-military affairs) paired skill, and flow analysis recommended at least 6 to 9 percent.
- Forty-one were extraneous—for example, fair-sharing estimated that 28 percent of 15W (weather) colonels needed paired skill in 36P (personnel), whereas flow analysis recommended none.
- Nine were unnecessarily high—for example, fair-sharing estimated that 14 percent of 21X (logistics) officers needed a paired skill in 63A (acquisition management), whereas flow analysis recommended at least 1 to 3 percent.
- Thirty-nine were too low—for example, fair-sharing estimated that 7 percent of 11S/12S (special operations) officers needed a paired skill in 16R (plans/programs), but flow analysis recommended at least 21 to 25 percent.

Moreover, fair-sharing failed to identify 33 of 91 pairings that flow analysis recommended—for example, paired skill in 33S (communications and information systems) for some 14N (intelligence) colonels, and in E&T (education and training) for some personnel colonels.

Table 4.8
Optimizations Exploit Flexibility: Recommended Percentage Alignments of Colonels with Positions' Requirements for Track and Experience Level

Required (for Position)		Fast Track			Not Fast Track				
Track	Experience Level	1st	2nd	Senior	1st	2nd	Senior	Total	Share of Positions
				Marginal Solution					
Fast	1st	30	22		33	16		100	6
	1st or 2nd	25	7	19	25	4	19	100	2
	2nd	17	16	22		40	6	100	4
	2nd or senior	20	12	22		17	29	100	2
	Senior		14	44			43	100	6
Fast total		17	16	21	13	15	19	100	20
Fast or not	1st	6	2		76	17		100	11
	1st or 2nd	2		1	66	8	23	100	5
	2nd	2	3	5	33	52	5	100	26
	2nd or senior	1	2	6	10	24	57	100	3
	Senior		3	21		29	47	100	8
	Any	5	2	5	52	18	18	100	27
Fast or not total		3	2	6	43	30	16	100	80
Grand total		6	5	9	37	27	16	100	100
				Preferred Solution					
Fast	1st	87	4		8	1		100	6
	1st or 2nd	84		7	8	0	0	100	2
	2nd	2	85	4		6	3	100	4
	2nd or senior	5	7	81		1	6	100	2
	Senior		1	93			5	100	6
Fast total		36	19	37	3	2	3	100	20
Fast or not	1st	10	1		88	2		100	11
	1st or 2nd	9	0	2	84	2	3	100	5
	2nd	1	20	3	5	71	1	100	26
	2nd or senior	1	2	16	8	16	58	100	3
	Senior		1	38		1	60	100	8
	Any	9	1	18	48	4	20	100	27
Fast or not total		5	7	12	36	26	15	100	80
Grand total		11	9	17	29	21	13	100	100

that were (flexibly) open to all experience levels, while the preferred solution recommended only 1 percent + 4 percent = 4 percent.[13]

Table 4.9 illustrates similar differentiation with respect to primary occupational skills, showing the alignments recommended for 106 positions open to all colonels with operational

[13] The numbers in Table 4.8 have been rounded to whole percentages. In the text's two cases that do not seem to add correctly, the more precise figures are 1.57 percent + 17.62 percent = 19.19 percent and 0.82 percent + 3.66 percent = 4.48 percent.

Table 4.9
Optimizations Exploit Flexibility: Recommended Percentage Alignments of Colonels with 106 Positions Open to All Operational Primary Skills (1YY)

Primary Skill Flexible?	Colonel's (Person's) Primary Skill		Marginal	Preferred
Substantial	11Y	Pilot	30.5	29.3
	RT	Any rated	14.4	11.7
Substantial total			45.0	41.0
Limited	11B/12B	Bomber	.4	1.0
	11B/12B/13SYC	Bomber or missile	1.3	.2
	11F/11H	Fighter or helicopter pilot	17.0	
	11S/12S	Special operations (SOF)		1.8
	13S	Space or missile	.5	7.9
	13SYA/B/D/E	Any space	5.7	4.5
	1YE	Experimental-test		1.0
	1YF	Fighter	4.2	5.8
	1YM	Mobility	.4	.8
	1YR	Reconnaissance		.1
	1YR/13B	Reconnaissance or ABM	.4	.1
	1YR/14N	Reconnaissance or intelligence	3.0	6.5
Limited total			32.8	29.6
No	11A	Airlift pilot		.6
	11F	Fighter pilot		1.4
	11R	Reconnaissance pilot	4.5	
	13A	Astronaut	2.0	
	13B	Air battle manager		.1
	13D	Control and recovery	1.6	.3
	13M	Airfield operations	5.5	5.6
	13SYA	Space satellite C2	2.5	4.9
	13SYB	Space lift	1.7	8.1
	13SYC	Missile	.2	3.4
	13SYD	Space surveillance	1.5	.6
	14N	Intelligence	2.3	3.7
	15W	Weather	6.5	6.6
No total			28.2	35.4
Grand total			106.0	106.0

(1YY) primary skills. For example, both solutions recommended that 13M (airfield operations) colonels fill about 5.5 of these 106 positions, whereas the preferred solution recommended notably more 13SYB (space lift) colonels (averaging more than eight) and the marginal solution notably fewer (averaging fewer than two).[14] Similar differentiation occurred for flexible paired skills—for example, Acq (any acquisition).

Table 4.9 also illustrates that (1) solutions from flow analysis reflected notably less flexibility than did the positions' requirements, and (2) the preferred solution retained less flexibility than the marginal solution. For the table's 106 positions, the two solutions recommended no colonels with flexibility in their primary skills as broad as 1YY, although sizable 11Y (pilot) and RT (rated) portions still reflected substantial flexibility. The solutions also recommended sizable numbers in skill categories with limited flexibility and in specific skills with no flexibility. Table 4.10 summarizes the overall prevalence of flexibility in primary occupation in the positions' requirements and in the two optimal solutions. For example, 16 percent of the positions required primary skills that were classified as having limited flexibility, compared with 18 percent of the marginal solution's recommended colonels and 24 percent of the preferred solution's recommended colonels.

Similarly, Table 4.11 summarizes the prevalence of flexibility in the positions' requirements and in the two optimal solutions' designations of paired skills. For example, 16 percent of the positions were inflexible ("no") in their requirements for a paired skill, compared with 24 percent of the marginal solution's colonels and 43 percent of the preferred solution's colonels. The pattern persists: Flow analysis found that developmental targets should be less flexible than position requirements alone indicate, and the preferred solution retained less flexibility than the marginal solution.

Table 4.12 shows how the flexibilities reflected in the positions' requirements migrated to different categories of flexibility in the flow optimizations' solutions. For example, in the sixth row for each solution, note (in the right-most column) that 17 percent of the 2,778 positions were characterized as substantially flexible for primary skill and completely flexible ("yes,"

Table 4.10
Flow Analysis Recommended Less Flexibility in Primary Skills

Primary Skill Flexible?	% of Positions	% of Flow Solution Inventory: Marginal	% of Flow Solution Inventory: Preferred
Yes	20		
Substantial	28	21	11
Limited	16	18	24
No	37	61	65
Total	100	100	100

NOTE: Columns may not sum to totals because of rounding.

---

[14] In contrast, fair-sharing would simply allocate those 106 positions to operational skills in proportion to their specific requirements—for example, because 5.4 times as many positions called for intelligence colonels (81 positions) as for weather officers (15 positions), then 5.4 times as many of the 106 positions would go to intelligence officers as to weather officers. But Table 4.9 shows that flow analysis recommended using intelligence officers notably less often than weather officers in these positions.

Table 4.11
Flow Analysis Recommended Less Flexibility in Paired Skills

Paired Skill Flexible?	% of Positions	% of Flow Solution Inventory	
		Marginal	Preferred
Yes	77	68	41
Substantial	5	4	8
Limited	3	4	8
No	16	24	43
Total	100	100	100

NOTE: Columns may not sum to totals because of rounding.

meaning no specific skill required) for a paired skill. For 36 percent of those positions, the marginal solution recommended aligning (or assigning) colonels whose primary skill was not flexible, and for 1 percent (out of that 36 percent), it recommended a paired skill that was not flexible. The corresponding percentages for the preferred solution were 37 percent and 4 percent, respectively. Table 4.12 reflects a general pattern: Numbers to the right of the (gray-shaded) principal diagonal represent shifts to less flexible skill categories. The shifts were substantial in both solutions and usually greater in the preferred solution.

It is worth noting that, although more colonels needed paired skills to obtain the preferred solution's benefits—that is, enhanced selectivity, better matches to positions' requirements for tracks and experience levels, and more graduating colonels with the skill pairs needed in GOs—the overall utilization[15] of paired skills would be lower, of course, because the numbers of positions needing those paired skills did not change. Table 4.13 reflects reductions of approximately 30 percentage points in utilization of the paired skills in total and for each primary skill category, according to the two solutions' recommended alignments of colonels with positions.

This observation naturally raises the question of whether the solutions also differed in their recommended utilization of primary skills.[16] Table 4.14 shows that rated colonels' primary skills were the least utilized (73 percent for rated versus 81 percent for all colonels, on average) in the marginal solution and the most utilized (87 percent for rated versus 81 percent for all) in the preferred solution. Utilization for rated colonels with paired skills was highest in both cases: 93 percent in the marginal solution and 91 percent in the preferred solution. So the large shift in rated utilization occurred among those without paired skills. At the same time, utilization of nonrated operations, logistics, and, to a lesser degree, support and OSI primary skills decreased notably in the preferred case. These shifts were due to changes in the mix of primary skills and their alignments with the positions open to more than one primary skill category.

---

[15] Utilization is the fraction of time that colonels would spend in jobs that call for their skill, or the fraction of colonels with a particular skill who would be in jobs that call for that skill. If a colonel's primary skill and paired skill were 11F (fighter pilot) and 63A (acquisition management), respectively, both would be utilized in a job that required RT (rated) primary skill and 6YY (acquisition or finance) paired skill, but neither would be utilized in a job open to all primary skills and that needed no paired skill.

[16] Positions open to any primary skill can be said not to utilize their incumbents' primary skills, because the experts declared such occupational restrictions unnecessary.

Table 4.12
Percentage of Positions Filled Using Inventory with Different Levels of Flexibility in Primary and Paired Skills

Required Primary Skill Flexible	Inv. Primary Flex. / Inv. Paired Skill Flex. / Rqd. Paired Skill Flex.	Substantial					Limited					No						
		Yes	Substantial	Limited	No	Subtotal	Yes	Substantial	Limited	No	Subtotal	Yes	Substantial	Limited	No	Subtotal	Total	Share of Positions
		Marginal Solution																
Yes	Yes	57	1	1	0	59	5		1	2	8	28	1	1	4	33	100	16
	Substantial		2	38		39						11	26	23	2	61	100	0
	Limited									8	8	17	22	19	33	92	100	0
	No				9	9				40	40	23		3	25	51	100	3
Yes total		47	1	1	2	51	4		1	8	12	27	1	2	7	37	100	20
Substantial	Yes	42	1	2	2	47	13		0	4	17	32	1	2	1	36	100	17
	Substantial		3	10	3	15		11	2	23	37	2	32	10	4	48	100	2
	Limited			16	40	56			4	3	7			19	18	37	100	1
	No				23	23				52	52				25	25	100	7
Substantial total		26	1	3	9	38	8	1	0	18	27	20	3	3	8	35	100	28
Limited	Yes						29	0	1	14	45	49	1	2	4	55	100	13
	Substantial							9	2	26	37		41		22	63	100	1
	Limited													33	67	100	100	0
	No									84	84	4			12	16	100	2
Limited total							22	1	1	25	50	38	4	2	7	50	100	16
No	Yes											89	2	3	5	100	100	31
	Substantial												82	12	5	100	100	1
	Limited													62	38	100	100	1
	No														100	100	100	3
No total												76	4	5	15	100	100	37
Marginal total		16	0	1	3	21	7	0	0	11	18	45	3	3	10	61	100	100

Table 4.12—Continued

Required Primary Skill Flexible	Inv. Primary Flex. → / Rqd. Paired Skill Flex. ↓ (Inv. Paired Skill Flex. →)	Substantial					Limited					No					Total	Share of Positions
		Yes	Substantial	Limited	No	Subtotal	Yes	Substantial	Limited	No	Subtotal	Yes	Substantial	Limited	No	Subtotal		
Preferred Solution																		
Yes	Yes	6		3	5	15	1	0	2	12	16	49	6	2	12	70	100	16
	Substantial			3		3	24			44	68		26	0	3	30	100	0
	Limited			7	2	10			2	42	44		25	5	17	46	100	0
	No				5	5				48	48	1		1	45	47	100	3
Yes total		5		3	5	13	1	0	2	18	21	41	6	2	17	66	100	20
Substantial	Yes	20	3	5	5	33	6	0	1	23	30	27	4	2	4	37	100	17
	Substantial		3		16	18		12	3	34	49	2	22	2	7	32	100	2
	Limited			11	60	71			4	5	9			5	16	20	100	1
	No				23	23				57	57				20	20	100	7
Substantial total		12	2	3	13	31	4	1	1	31	37	17	4	2	9	32	100	28
Limited	Yes						12	4	1	38	55	22	5	7	10	45	100	13
	Substantial							17	1	16	34		41		25	66	100	1
	Limited									33	33			33	33	67	100	0
	No									82	82			3	16	18	100	2
Limited total							9	4	1	43	57	17	7	6	12	43	100	16
No	Yes											58	6	10	26	100	100	31
	Substantial												84	10	6	100	100	1
	Limited													65	35	100	100	1
	No														100	100	100	3
No total												49	8	11	32	100	100	37
Preferred total		4	1	2	5	11	3	1	1	19	24	33	6	6	20	65	100	100

Table 4.13
O-6 Positions' Percentage Utilization of Aligned Colonels' Paired Skills

Primary Skill Category	Marginal Solution	Preferred Solution
Rated operations	70	43
Nonrated operations	78	46
Logistics	56	23
Support and OSI	54	21
Acquisition and finance	71	40
Total	68	38

NOTE: Utilization = percentage of inventory assigned to jobs that require paired skills

Table 4.14
O-6 Positions' Percentage Utilization of Aligned Colonels' Primary Skills

Primary Skill Category	Paired Skill?	Marginal Solution	Preferred Solution
Rated	Yes	93	91
	No	67	83
	Total	73	87
Nonrated operations	Yes	92	81
	No	97	58
	Total	94	79
Logistics	Yes	83	78
	No	96	73
	Total	91	76
Support and OSI	Yes	71	85
	No	86	69
	Total	83	75
Acquisition and finance	Yes	89	81
	No	82	84
	Total	85	82
Total	Yes	88	83
	No	78	77
	Total	81	81

Below, we consider those changes at greater length, noting now only that rated colonels contributed 61 percent of those whose primary skill was not utilized in the marginal solution, but only 37 percent in the preferred solution. It is also noteworthy that in both solutions, the utilization of primary skills tended to be higher for colonels with paired skills—about 9 percentage points higher in the marginal solution[17] and 6 percentage points in the preferred solution.[18]

Primary Skill Shifts

During 2005, this research helped create percentage goals for the development of paired skills within the Air Force's primary line occupations, but tacitly it offered insights about the mix of primary skills themselves. Figure 4.1 shows the mixes of primary skill categories reflected in 2002's authorizations,[19] the functional experts' specification of requirements,[20] the actual O-6 force during FY 2005,[21] and the two model solutions. Note especially the considerable

Figure 4.1
Mixes of Primary Skill Categories in the Colonel Force

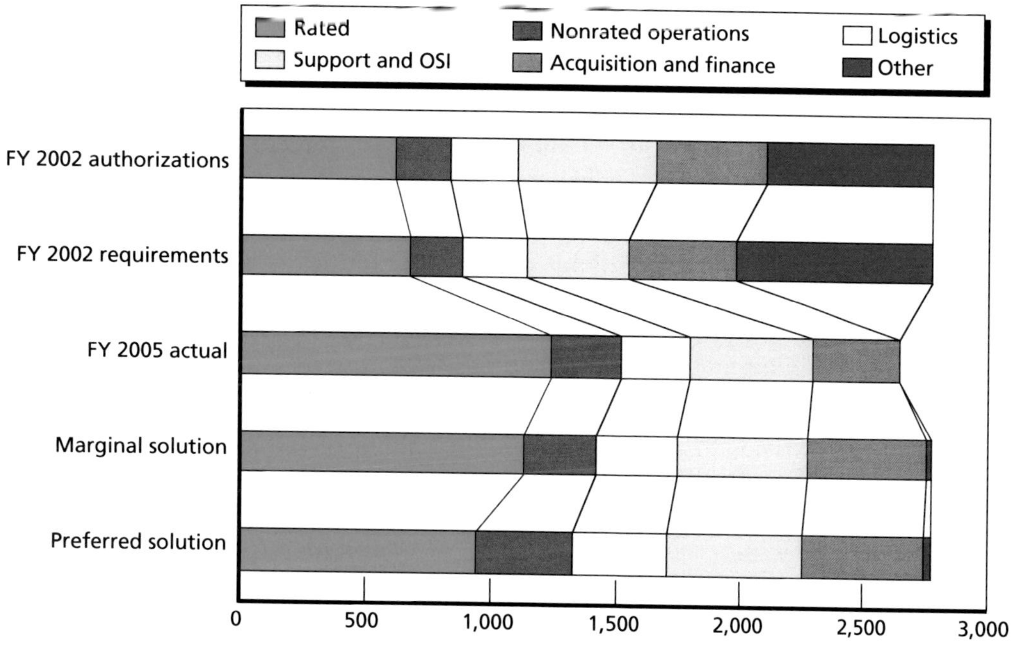

RAND *TR759-4.1*

[17] Table 4.14 portrays a difference of 88 percent – 78 percent = 10 percent for colonels with paired skills, but more accurate figures are 87.5 percent – 78.3 percent = 9.2 percent, which rounds to 9 percent.

[18] The underlying cause in both solutions is that positions open to any primary skill required paired skills less often: 17 percent of the positions open to any primary skill required a paired skill, versus 25 percent of the rest.

[19] The sizable "other" category represents positions authorized in generic AFSCs or reporting identifiers—for example, 16R (planning and programming), 16G (operations staff officer), 81T (instructor), and 91C (commander)—that are not within the primary occupational skill categories.

[20] Here "other" includes positions that the experts said could be filled by colonels from more than one specific primary skill category.

[21] AF/DPXF provided FY 2005's actual breakout of so-called core AFSCs. The O-6 force was somewhat smaller in FY 2005 than in FY 2002 to which the other four bars in the figure pertain. Moreover, actual assigned personnel often fall short of authorized positions, the basis for the other bars.

difference between the actual mix during FY 2005 and the preferred solution's mix. The actual mix included 47 percent rated, 11 percent nonrated operations, 10 percent logistics, 19 percent support and OSI, and 13 percent acquisition and finance colonels. The preferred solution recommended 34 percent rated, 14 percent nonrated operations, 14 percent logistics, 20 percent support and OSI, 18 percent acquisition and finance, and 1 percent other[22] colonels, proposing a noteworthy shift from rated to nonrated skills. Why? Recall that the optimizations try to create primary skill mixes as similar as possible to a reference or target mix, and here we used the FY 2005 O-6 core AFSC force as that target mix. Consequently, the recommended mixes differ from FY 2005's mix because other goals had higher priorities, specifically meeting or surpassing the requirements for incoming GOs,[23] minimizing shortfalls in selectivity, and minimizing the number of new colonels with paired skills. Lacking information about their paired skills, tracks, and experience levels, we could not assess how nearly FY 2005's actual force met the constraints and objective values the optimizations achieved. We only know that, mathematically, it proved impossible to stay closer to FY 2005's actual mix of primary skills without either degrading the steady-state pool of colonels available for promotion to GO, accepting selectivity shortfalls below minimum targets when O-6 vacancies occur, or requiring more new colonels to bring paired skills. Further research could examine this issue further, investigating the degree to which other achievable goals could not be met if rated colonels remain so prevalent over time. Preliminary evidence from this work suggests that, with more rated colonels than recommended, utilization of their rated primary skills will be lower, shortfalls from selectivity goals will occur, more new colonels will need paired skills, or the mix of candidates available for promotion to GO will be inadequate. The optimizations recommended reducing rated colonels by about 15 to 25 percent, increasing support and OSI colonels by about 5 to 10 percent, and increasing acquisition and finance colonels by about 40 to 50 percent.

The optimizations recommended few significant changes in the mixes of primary skills within the primary skill categories, however. For the most part, FY 2005's actual number of colonels in each primary skill fell between the numbers recommended in the marginal and preferred optimization solutions or fairly near that range. Noteworthy relative increases were recommended mainly in 13D (control and recovery), 35P (public affairs), and 61S (scientist), and a noteworthy relative decrease was recommended only in 62E (developmental engineering).

Shifts in Recommended Paired Skills

As noted, we did not try to assess the mix of paired skills in FY 2005's 2,648 colonels. Nevertheless, it is illuminating to highlight differences in the mixes of paired skills recommended in the marginal and preferred optimization solutions. Table 4.15 lists the 20 skills that increased the most from the marginal to the preferred solution, many of them approximately doubling. The largest increases tended to be in the paired skills that were largest in the first place: APE (aerospace power employment), 16R (plans/programs), Acq and 63A (acquisition), and 16P (political-mililitary affairs). Table 4.16 lists the 20 skill pairings (primary skills and paired skills)

---

22 In the optimization solutions, "other" represented a few colonels that the model needed for positions with unknown skill requirements plus a few where it proved unnecessary to designate just one skill category.

23 Recall that meeting or surpassing the requirements for incoming GOs forms a family of constraints in the optimization model. Constraints enjoy even higher priorities than the objective functions.

Table 4.15
Top 20 Increases in Paired Skills: Preferred Versus Marginal Solution

Paired Skill		Number in Solution		Increase	
		Marginal	Preferred	Number	Percentage
APE	Aerospace power employment	111.0	219.6	108.6	98
16R	Plans/programs	101.9	184.1	82.2	81
Acq	Any acquisition	65.3	121.2	56.0	86
16P	International political-military affairs	49.0	97.3	48.3	99
63A	Acquisition management	86.1	130.7	44.7	52
33S	Communications and information systems	32.3	64.7	32.4	100
E&T	Education and training	29.0	60.1	31.2	108
13S	Space or missile	30.8	61.3	30.4	99
IO	Information operations	55.0	82.3	27.3	50
36P	Personnel	23.6	46.5	22.9	97
MO	Mobility operations	17.2	34.3	17.2	100
2YY	Any logistics	16.6	33.4	16.7	100
6YY	Acquisition/financial management	16.1	32.1	15.9	99
13SYA	Space satellite C2	14.5	26.4	11.9	82
13SYB	Space lift	13.6	25.5	11.9	87
21MYA	Munitions and missile maintenance, missile	13.6	23.9	10.3	76
36P/38M	Personnel or manpower	9.9	19.8	9.9	100
16P/16R	Plans/programs or international political-military affairs	9.4	18.9	9.4	100
21R	Logistics readiness	9.2	18.5	9.2	100
13SYC	Missile	9.3	18.1	8.8	95

that increased the most, many of them also approximately doubling. By far the largest total increase was in the number of 1YF (fighter) specialists with a paired skill in APE. It seems noteworthy, however, that more than half of Table 4.16's increases were in nonrated primary skills, mostly in the acquisition and logistics categories.

Selectivity Levels

For both sets of parameter values, the optimization found solutions meeting the minimum selectivity requirements: at least 2.0 in the marginal case and at least 3.0 in the preferred case. Table 4.17 lists the primary and paired skills where the solutions just barely met the selectivity goals. It seems noteworthy that all of the requirements where selectivity limits were barely met were indifferent about experience level (colonels in any experience tier were acceptable) and about track (either fast-track or not-fast-track colonels were acceptable)—that is, they were

Table 4.16
Top 20 Increases in Pairings: Primary and Paired Skills in the Marginal and Preferred Solutions

Primary Skill		Paired Skill		Solution		Increase	
				Marginal	Preferred	Number	Percentage
1YF	Fighter	APE	Aerospace power employment	48.3	96.6	48.3	100
21R	Logistics readiness	16R	Plans/programs	1.3	16.7	15.4	1,203
1YM	Mobility	16R	Plans/programs	12.1	26.9	14.8	122
61S	Scientist	63A	Acquisition management	9.2	23.3	14.2	155
1YF	Fighter	16P	International political-military affairs	13.1	26.3	13.1	100
Acq	Any acquisition	13SYA	Space satellite C2	14.5	26.4	11.9	82
Acq	Any acquisition	13SYB	Space lift	13.6	25.5	11.9	87
14N	Intelligence	IO	Information operations	15.0	26.5	11.6	77
1YM	Mobility	APE	Aerospace power employment	11.3	22.7	11.3	100
35P	Public affairs	16P	International political-military affairs	11.0	21.6	10.6	97
21MYB	Munitions and missile maintenance, space lift	33S	Communications and information systems	10.4	20.9	10.5	101
13SYC	Missile	21MYA	Munitions and missile maintenance, missile	13.6	23.9	10.3	76
11S/12S	Special operations	APE	Aerospace power employment	10.0	20.1	10.0	100
21B	Equipment maintenance	E&T	Education and training	8.3	18.1	9.8	118
11F	Fighter pilot	16R	Plans/programs	9.4	19.1	9.6	102
21G	Logistics plans	2YY	Any logistics	9.4	18.9	9.4	100
63A	Acquisition management	16P/ 16R	Plans/programs or international political-military affairs	9.4	18.9	9.4	100
21B	Equipment maintenance	63A	Acquisition management	9.8	19.1	9.3	95
13SYB	Space lift	Acq	Any acquisition	9.6	18.9	9.3	97
1YM	Mobility	MO	Mobility operations	9.1	18.1	9.1	100

flexible about experience and track. Although several groups had more than one position, the lowest selectivity for these groups applied to only the last position to be filled. Hence, expected selectivity would be as low as 2.0 or scarcely higher for only 16 positions in the marginal solution, and it would be as low as 3.0 or scarcely higher for only 12 positions in the preferred solution. Overall, selectivity would average more than 230 colonels with the necessary primary and paired skills per opening under both the marginal and preferred solutions, exceeding 1,000 for 299 positions in both cases, the majority of those positions open to any primary skill, needing

Table 4.17
Skill Pairings Where Solutions Barely Met Selectivity Minimums

Primary Skill		Paired Skill		Solution	
				Marginal	Preferred
11B/12B/13SYC	Bomber or missile	16R	Plans/programs	x	
13S	Space or missile	16P	International political-military affairs	x	
13S	Space or missile	IO	Information operations	x	x
13SYB	Space lift	16R	Plans/programs	x	x
14N	Intelligence	APE	Aerospace power employment	x	
14N/33Y	Intelligence or communications	14N/33Y	Intelligence or communications	x	x
1YR	Reconnaissance	Acq	Any acquisition	x	x
1YY	Any operations	14N	Intelligence	x	
35B	Band	None	None	x	x
35P	Public affairs	16R	Plans/programs	x	
62E	Developmental engineering	13S/14N	Space, missile, or intelligence		x
62E	Developmental engineering	13SYB/C	Space lift or missile	x	x
63A	Acquisition management	13B	Air battle manager	x	x
63A	Acquisition management	65F	Financial management	x	x
6YY	Acquisition/financial management	33Y	Communications	x	x
FB	Fighter or bomber	IO	Information operations	x	x
Unknown	Unknown	Unknown	Unknown	x	x

no paired skill, accepting either fast-track or not-fast-track colonels, and with some flexibility in the required experience level.

Figure 4.2 plots the numbers of positions that would experience lower average selectivities under the two solutions. The disparity was greater at the lowest selectivities, of course. The marginal solution left 64 positions with average selectivities below 3.0, whereas the preferred solution left none. The marginal solution left a total of 64 + 76 + 75 + 43 = 278 positions with average selectivities below 6.0, whereas the preferred solution left only 57.

Figure 4.2
Numbers of Positions with Lower Average Selectivities

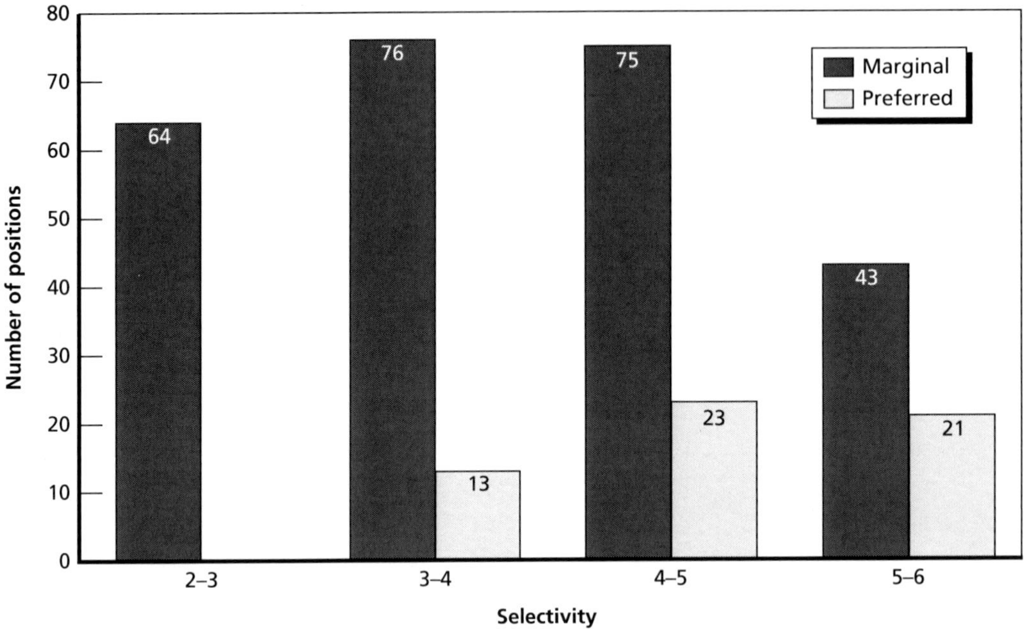

NOTE: Selectivity is the average number of qualified colonels available when an opening occurs.
RAND *TR759-4.2*

CHAPTER FIVE

Deriving Developmental Floors for Officer Development Teams

Air Staff and AFPC members of the working group who helped develop and review this analysis believed that the Air Force's officer development teams could not yet cope with some of the categories and details that the flow analysis addressed. For example, they viewed as too broad the flexible RT (rated) category that cut across the CAF, MAF, and SOF development teams, and, within the CAF team's scope, they viewed as too narrow the distinctions among 11B (bomber pilots), 11B/12B (bomber pilots or navigators), FB (fighter or bomber) specialists, and 13B (air battle managers). We believed that the development teams eventually could and should address the flexible categories because they would provide genuinely valuable options—for example, in one year it may be easier to rely more on the MAF for some paired skills and in another year easier to rely more on the CAF or SOF. We also believed that the teams should address the finer distinctions because they are meaningful—for example, rated fighter, bomber, reconnaissance, and air battle managers cannot always substitute for each other, even though all are overseen by the CAF development team.

We relieved the Headquarters and AFPC staffs' concerns by adjusting the flow model's marginal and preferred floors so that their skill boundaries coincided with development teams' boundaries. Specifically, we derived aggregate but separate marginal and preferred floors for the CAF, MAF, and SOF rated development teams and for the 61S (scientist), 62E (developmental engineering), 63A (acquisition management), 64P (contracting), and 65X (finance) development teams within the broad acquisition/finance category.

Before describing how we made those adjustments, it seems useful to summarize an alternative approach that we believed would be more beneficial. We could not adopt the alternative in the moment because time was too short and because Air Force staff officers favored keeping things relatively simple while the development teams began using quantitative floors to guide their vectoring of officers into paired skills.

A Better Way to Target Developmental Objectives: Exploit Development Already Completed and Available Development Opportunities

We perceived the conceptual difficulty to be more in allocating the flexibility that remained in the flow model's skill recommendations than in addressing specific differences within a development team's purview. For example, the 61S, 62E, 63A, and 64P development teams would need to coordinate their planning to ensure meeting the preferred solution's target of about 11 new generic Acq (acquisition) colonels per year, and the CAF, MAF, and SOF development teams would need to coordinate their planning to ensure meeting the preferred solution's target of about six new generic RT (rated) colonels per year. Cross-DT coordination seemed more difficult than addressing distinctions entirely within one development team's scope. An example of the latter would be ensuring that enough 61SYAs (scientific analysts) within the 61S (scientist) career field developed paired skill in 13S (space and missile operations) or that enough 11Fs (fighter pilots) within the CAF developed paired skill in 16R (plans/programs).

Addressing cross-DT issues might prove relatively straightforward in practice if the Air Force tracked officers' experience in the various paired skills—for example, how much experience each 61SYA (scientific analyst) officer had in space and missile operations and how much each fighter pilot had in plans/programs.[1] For instance, if enough 63As (acquisition managers) in a cohort already had a paired skill in 13SYB (space lift)—where the marginal and preferred solutions, respectively, recommended averaging at least 2.3 and 4.3 new generic Acq (acquisition) colonels per year—then no 61S (scientist), 62E (developmental engineering), or 64P (contracting) members of that cohort would need the 13SYB paired skill. Similarly, if enough 11S/12S (SOF) officers in a cohort had a paired skill in 14N (intelligence)—where the marginal and preferred solutions, respectively, recommended averaging at least 1.9 and 2.4 new generic RT (rated) colonels per year—no additional CAF or MAF members of that cohort would need the 14N paired skill. For each such generic occupational category, the Air Force could see and take credit for any development already completed across officers in the range of acceptable career fields, rather than tagging each eligible career field with developing the targeted paired skill in some of its officers.

Further, if too few members of the cohort in a targeted generic primary skill had developed a targeted paired skill, the Air Force could use data about the positions that contribute to the development of that paired skill. For example, if relatively more 62E (developmental engineering) positions gave experience in 13SYB (space lift), then more of the responsibility for preparing candidates to meet or exceed the marginal and preferred minimums of at least, respectively, 2.3 and 4.3 new generic Acq (acquisition) colonels per year with a paired skill in 13SYB (space lift) could go to the 62E development team rather than being split arbitrarily among the 61S, 62E, 63A, and 64P teams. For another example, if relatively more 13B (air battle management) positions naturally gave experience in IO (information operations), then more of the responsibility for preparing candidates to meet or exceed the marginal and preferred minimums of at least, respectively, 0.6 and 1.2 new generic RT (rated) colonels per year with a paired skill in IO could go to the CAF development team rather than being split arbitrarily among the CAF, MAF, and SOF development teams. This argues for a database that would characterize the experiences that officers accrue from holding different Air Force positions.[2]

---

1 An appropriate data system could track officers' experience in different paired skills and also whether officers were "certified" (or the level of certification earned) in each paired skill. In 2005, AFPC had roughed out a database telling whether each officer had worked at least 12 months in each paired skill. Twelve months of experience is far short of Air Force senior leaders' initial criteria for earning paired skills (or secondary occupational competencies), but the database represented a good beginning.

2 AFPC derived the rough database mentioned in the previous footnote by reviewing officers' past positions and registering the experiences gained, based mainly on the positions' authorized AFSCs. But it seems straightforward to tap additional information (e.g., organizational affiliations and functional account codes) in Air Force personnel records to discern and register experience more comprehensively and accurately. RAND has demonstrated this practicality in previous studies—for example, in Vernez et al. (2006) for space and missile operations officers (13S), in Brauner et al. (2009) for intelligence officers (14N), and in a comparison study (unpublished) with GO inflow targets of the primary and paired skills found in successive pools of colonels who were viewed as competitive for promotion to GO. The Air Force Space Command main-

Indeed, reliable and current databases about (a) officers' experience in paired skills and (b) positions' contributions to paired skills would facilitate both the resolution of floors that cut across development teams and the handling of unmet floors within a development team's scope. The key would be to track each officer's progress toward developing paired skills, to compare each cohort's development with each pertinent floor, to identify any shortfalls, and to identify the best ways of closing any gaps.

Lacking time and resources to test that better approach, however, we opted instead to transform the model-optimized floors into DT-level floors by subdividing and allocating floors for flexible inventory categories, and cross-DT floors, and aggregating some detailed, within-DT floors, aiming to balance the DTs' needs to develop officers with paired skills.

Balancing Development Teams' Floors for Paired Skills

Table 5.1 shows the primary skills in the optimal solutions that "belonged to" each development team. Note that many of the flexible primary skill groups could be the responsibility of more than one development team—for example, 11Y (pilot), RT (rated), 11B/12B/13SYC (bomber or missile), or Acq (any acquisition). As we noted in Chapter Four before summarizing the percentage targets within the five broad skill categories, we allocated each of four occupationally flexible inventories to one skill category, as follows:

- 11B/12B/13SYC (bomber or missile) went to 11B/12B (bomber) in the rated category.
- 1YR/14N (reconnaissance or intelligence) went to 14N (intelligence) in the nonrated operations category.
- 14N/33S (intelligence or communications/information systems) went to 33S (communications/information systems) in the support/OSI category.
- Acq/2YY (acquisition or logistics) went to 2YY (logistics) in the logistics category.

That left sizable flexible minimums within two categories. Some 53 percent of the marginal solution's rated entrants and 30 percent of the preferred solution's rated entrants were still in flexible primary groups such as RT (any rated) or 11Y (pilot), not specific to one development team. And 12 percent and 22 percent, respectively, of the marginal and preferred solutions' entrants in the acquisition and finance category were still in flexible primary groups such as 6YY (acquisition and finance) or Acq (any acquisition). Moreover, we thought it might help (a) the 21X (logistics) development team to see floors for 21M (maintenance) versus 21R (logistics readiness) because 16 percent and 6 percent of its marginal and preferred inflows remained flexible, respectively, and (b) the 13S (space and missile operations) development team to see floors for its shredouts because about 40 percent of its entrants were in flexible categories such as 13S (space or missile) or 13SYA/B/D/E (any space). We used the same steps to balance the paired skills within these two DTs as to balance them across the three rated DTs and across the five acquisition and finance DTs.

---

tains and uses such a database routinely for its officer, enlisted, and civilian professionals, concentrating on experiences within its occupational domain.

Table 5.1
Primary Skills Belonging to Each Development Team

		Avg. Entrants per Year		Development Team (DT)																						
Primary Skill		Marg.	Pref.	CAF	MAF	SOF	13D	13M	13S	14N	15W	21X	31P	32E	33S	34M	35X	37F	61S	62E	63A	64P	65X	71S	None	# of DTs
11A	Airlift pilot	15.3	11.1		x																					1
11B	Bomber pilot	1.2	2.4	x																						1
11B/12B	Bomber	4.7	6.5	x																						1
11B/12B/ 13SYC	Bomber or missile	.2	.5	x					x																	2
11E	Experimental-test pilot	1.2	2.3	x	x	x																				3
11F	Fighter pilot	22.6	22.9	x																						1
11F/11B	Fighter or bomber pilot	5.2		x																						1
11F/11H	Fighter or helicopter pilot	8.0	5.9	x		x																				2
11H	Helicopter pilot	1.3	2.6			x																				1
11H/11S/ 12S	Helicopter pilot or SOF	2.1	.2			x																				1
11R	Reconnais-sance pilot	1.4	2.7	x																						1
11S/12S	Special operations	5.9	10.0			x																				1
11Y	Pilot	78.6	25.2	x	x	x																				3
13A	Astronaut	2.5	4.6	x	x	x																				3
13B	Air battle manager	5.5	3.2	x																						1
13D	Control and recovery	1.3	2.7				x																			1
13M	Airfield operations	1.2	2.3					x																		1
13S	Space or missile	5.5	6.5						x																	1
13SYA	Space satellite C2	1.4	2.7						x																	1
13SYA/B/ D/E	Any space	2.8	5.5						x																	1

Table 5.1—Continued

Primary Skill		Avg. Entrants per Year		Development Team (DT)																						
		Marg.	Pref.	CAF	MAF	SOF	13D	13M	13S	14N	15W	21X	31P	32E	33S	34M	35X	37F	61S	62E	63A	64P	65X	71S	None	# of DTs
13SYA/ D/E	Space satellite C2, surveillance, or warning	.1							x																	1
13SYB	Space lift	3.3	6.5						x																	1
13SYC	Missile	5.6	6.6						x																	1
13SYD	Space surveillance	1.3	2.4						x																	1
14N	Intelligence	19.7	18.8							x																1
14N/ 33S	Intelligence or communications/ information systems	.2								x					x											2
15W	Weather	3.5	3.8								x															1
1YE	Experimental-test	1.0	1.3	x	x	x																				3
1YF	Fighter	10.2	20.5	x																						1
1YF/ 1YM	Fighter or mobility	.2		x	x																					2
1YM	Mobility	6.7	14.0		x																					1
1YM/11S/ 12S	Mobility or SOF	.2			x	x																				2
1YR	Reconnais-sance	.6	.9	x																						1
1YR/13B	Reconnais-sance or ABM	.7	1.4	x																						1
1YR/14N	Reconnais-sance or intelligence	1.3	2.7	x						x																2
1YT	Tanker	4.6	5.8		x																					1
21A	Aircraft maintenance	1.4	2.9									x														1
21A/B/M	Maintenance	1.0	2.1									x														1
21B	Equipment maintenance	21.2	28.2									x														1
21B/21R	Equipment maint or logistics readiness	6.4	.8									x														1

Table 5.1—Continued

Primary Skill		Avg. Entrants per Year		Development Team (DT)																						
		Marg.	Pref.	CAF	MAF	SOF	13D	13M	13S	14N	15W	21X	31P	32E	33S	34M	35X	37F	61S	62E	63A	64P	65X	71S	None	# of DTs
21G	Logistics plans	2.7	5.5									x														1
21M	Munitions and missile maintenance	1.6	3.2									x														1
21MYA	Munitions and missile maintenance, missile	2.0	3.9									x														1
21MYB	Munitions and missile maintenance, space lift	1.6	3.3									x														1
21R	Logistics readiness	11.2	5.4									x														1
21S	Supply	1.4	2.7									x														1
21T	Transportation	1.4	2.7									x														1
2YY	Any logistics	1.1	.1									x														1
31P	Security forces	7.0	11.5										x													1
32E	Civil engineering	13.6	18.3											x												1
33Y	Communications and information systems	30.0	21.6												x											1
34M	Services	4.3	7.4													x										1
35B	Band	.6	1.0														x									1
35P	Public affairs	3.7	5.9														x									1
36P	Personnel	19.5	7.8															x								1
36P/38M	Personnel or manpower	2.4	4.7															x								1
38M	Manpower	2.1	3.4															x								1
61S	Scientist	6.4	8.9																x							1
61S/62E	Scientist or developmental engineering	1.3	1.9																x	x						2
61SYA	Analytical scientist	1.2	2.3																x							1
62E	Developmental engineering	9.9	6.6																	x						1

Table 5.1—Continued

		Avg. Entrants per Year		Development Team (DT)																						
Primary Skill		Marg.	Pref.	CAF	MAF	SOF	13D	13M	13S	14N	15W	21X	31P	32E	33S	34M	35X	37F	61S	62E	63A	64P	65X	71S	None	# of DTs
63A	Acquisition management	35.3	15.6																		x					1
64P	Contracting	8.5	12.9																			x				1
65F	Financial management	9.3	15.7																				x			1
65W	Cost analysis	1.2	2.3																				x			1
6YY	Acquisition/ financial management	2.5	5.1																x	x	x	x	x			5
71S	Special investigations	4.1	8.0																					x		1
Acq	Any acquisition	5.8	10.9																x	x	x	x				4
Acq/2YY	Any acquisition or any logistics	1.3	2.7									x							x	x	x	x				5
FB	Fighter or bomber		.8	x																						1
FB/1YM	Fighter, bomber, or mobility	.3		x	x																					2
FB/1YM/ 11S/12S	Fighter, bomber, mobility, or SOF	.1		x	x	x																				3
RT	Any rated	5.2	6.3	x	x	x																				3
RT not 13B	Any rated except ABM	1.2		x	x	x																				3
Unknown	Unknown	1.0	1.3																						x	1
Grand Total		457.9	448.5																							

Those steps used a straightforward nonlinear optimization mechanism:

- Decision variables: number of flexible entrants with each combination of primary and paired skills and on each track allocated to each DT or primary eligible skill—for example, the number with each paired skill and designated as RT (rated) allocated to the CAF team, or the number with each paired skill and designated as 13SYA/B/D/E (any space) allocated to 13SYB (space lift)—without changing the paired skill or track.
- Minimize the weighted sum of the relevant DTs' squared deviations from their average composite percentage with each paired skill, including "none" as one of the paired skills. That is, try to give the affected DTs similar mixes of paired skills.

For the preferred solution, Figure 5.1 illustrates how the allocation balanced the rated DTs' burdens for developing future new colonels with paired skills, by allocating the flexible 30 percent of rated entrants to the CAF, MAF, and SOF. Before the allocation, 79 percent of the new colonels specifically needed from SOF, 66 percent of those specifically needed from CAF, and 45 percent of those specifically needed from MAF needed paired skills, compared with only 31 percent of those who could come from more than one of those communities. After the allocation, all three communities were charged with producing about the same percentages of new colonels with paired skills: 51 percent for MAF and 53 percent each for CAF and SOF.

This balancing approach eliminated flexibility and masked differences that matter. We recommended avoiding it in the future by creating, maintaining, and exploiting databases of officers' accumulating progress toward paired skills and of positions' contributions to paired skills. Then development teams could make additional distinctions that mattered and, with help from AFPC, tell whether/when/how they should coordinate with respect to any flexible category that affected more than one development team.

The Floors

We end this chapter with tables that summarize the percentage floors derived for the various developmental teams. Some emerged from the balancing mechanism described above, and others came straight from the original flow analyses. These tables are generally simpler than Chapter Four's Tables 4.3–4.7, which helped introduce the detailed marginal and preferred solutions.

Rated Floors

Figure 5.1 portrays somewhat different mixes of paired skills in the three rated DTs' floors. Arranging the paired skills from highest to lowest floors, Table 5.2 lists the results drawn using the balancing mechanism.

- The three DTs' percentage floors were nearly the same for the paired skills 6YY (acquisition or finance), 14N (intelligence), 2YY/63A (any logistics or acquisition management), EW (electronic warfare), and IO (information operations).

Figure 5.1
Illustration: Balancing the Preferred Solution's Skill-Pairing Floors for the Rated Development Teams

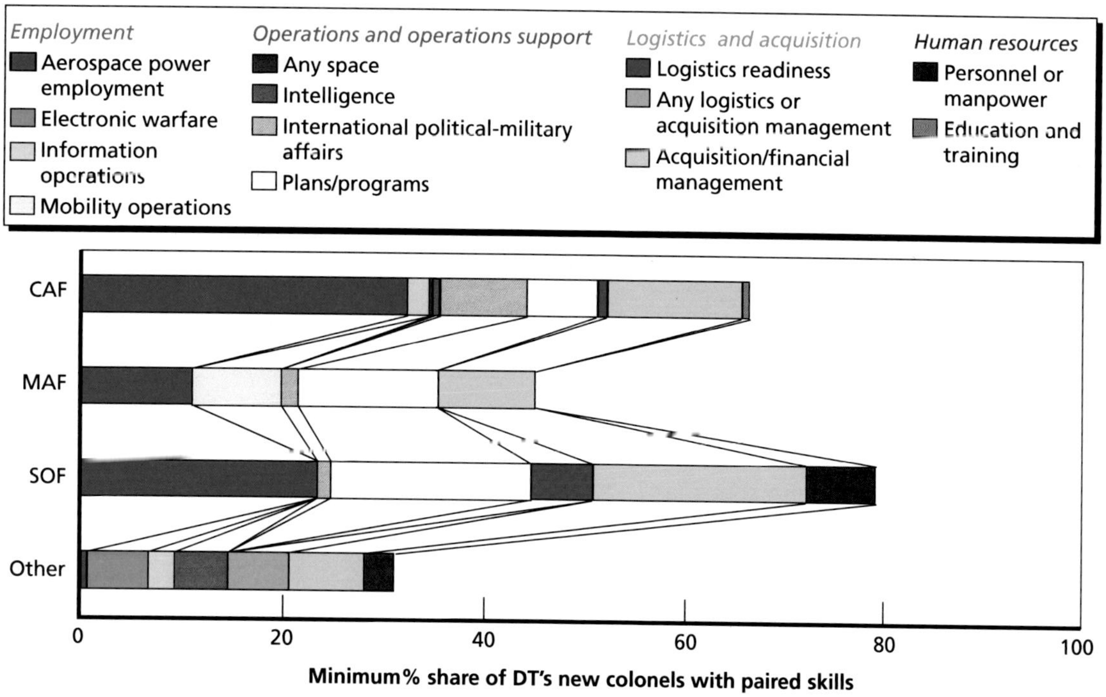

(a) *Before* allocating the 30 percent of rated total that were open to multiple rated DTs.

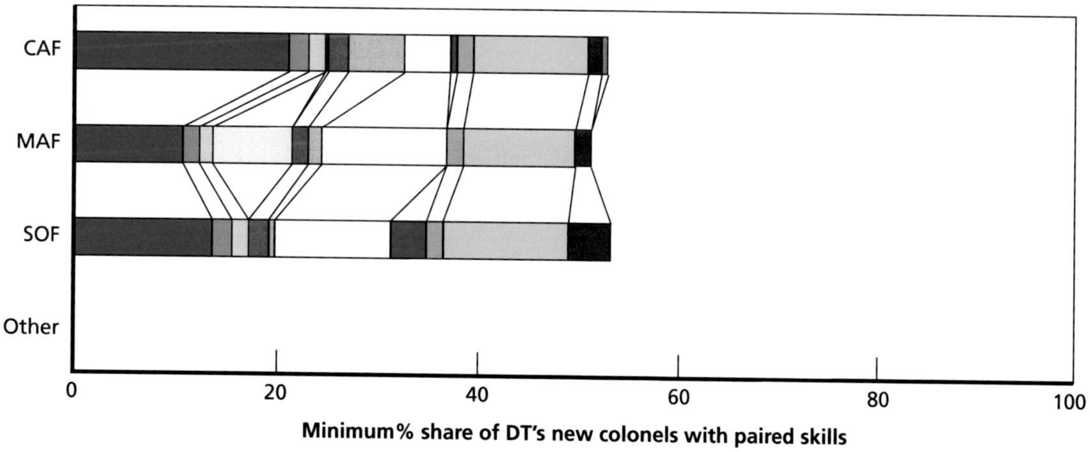

(b) *After* allocating the 30 percent of rated total that were open to multiple rated DTs.

NOTE: In the preferred solution, 30 percent of the new rated colonels could come from more than one rated DT, and 69 percent of this flexible group needed no paired skill. Not surprisingly, the balancing mechanism allocated to the three DTs far more entrants that did not need paired skills than entrants that did.

RAND *TR759-5.1*

- CAF's floors were somewhat higher than the other rated DTs' for the paired skills APE (aerospace power employment), 16P (political-military affairs), E&T (education and training), and 13SYA/B/D/E (any space), and somewhat lower for 16R (plans and programs), and 36P/38M (personnel or manpower).

Table 5.2
Balanced Percentage Floors for the Rated Development Teams

Paired Skill		CAF		MAF		SOF		All Rated Forces	
		Marginal	Preferred	Marginal	Preferred	Marginal	Preferred	Marginal	Preferred
APE	Aerospace power employment	9	21	4	11	5	14	7	18
6YY	Acquisition or finance	6	11	6	11	6	12	6	12
16R	Plans/programs	3	4	4	12	6	11	4	7
16P	International political-military affairs	2	6	1	1	.3	1	2	4
14N	Intelligence	1	2	1	2	1	2	1	2
2YY/63A	Any logistics or acquisition management	1	2	1	2	1	2	1	2
EW	Electronic warfare	1	2	1	2	1	2	1	2
MO	Mobility operations			3	8			1	2
IO	Information operations	1	2	1	2	1	2	1	2
36P/38M	Personnel or manpower	.5	1	1	2	2	4	1	2
21R	Logistics readiness	.3	.7			1	4	.4	1
E&T	Education and training	.3	.7					.2	.4
13SYA/B/D/E	Any space	.1	.2					.05	.1
Minimum with paired skill		25	53	21	51	23	53	24	53

- The MAF did not need such a large share with a paired skill in APE (aerospace power employment), but only the MAF needed to produce new colonels with paired skill in MO (mobility operations).[3]
- Balancing recommended that new SOF colonels include somewhat larger shares with paired skills in 16R (plans and programs), 36P/38M (personnel/manpower), and 21R (logistics readiness).

Some of the percentages in Table 5.2 and in similar tables for other career fields are rather small. How to interpret them? Remember that the tables' numbers represent minimum percentages of long-run averages, not necessarily minimum percentages of each year's new colonels. For example, if an average of about 100 new CAF colonels were anticipated per year, then Table 5.2's lower limit of 0.3 to 0.7 percent for a paired skill in 21R (logistics readiness) would translate to about one new such CAF colonel every two or three years.

---

[3] Mobility operations is a form of aerospace power employment, of course. Nevertheless, beginning from our early analysis for the GO and SES force, Air Force leaders distinguished the two, with the understanding that APE meant the employment of combat forces and MO meant the employment of mobility forces. Table 5.2 indicates that those needing a paired skill in either APE or MO added to nearly the same shares of new CAF and MAF colonels, somewhat larger shares than for new SOF colonels.

Floors for Nonrated Operations

Table 5.3 shows that the nonrated operations career fields' floors for paired skills had little in common. As noted previously, new colonels from 13D (control and recovery) needed no paired skills, and those from 13M (airfield operations) and 15W (weather) needed only one: 33S (communications and information systems) for 13M and 16R (plans and programs) for 15W. 13S (space and missile operations) and 14N (intelligence) needed a wider variety of paired skills, especially 13S. Before considering 13S in more detail, we observe that the paired skills for 14N seemed reasonable: IO (information operations) was the largest, APE (aerospace power

Table 5.3
Percentage Floors for Nonrated Operations Development Teams

		13D		13M		13S		14N		15W			
		Control and Recovery		Airfield Operations		Space and Missile Operations		Intelligence		Weather		All Nonrated Operations	
Paired Skill		Marg.	Pref.	Marg.	Pref.	Marg.	Pref.	Marg.	Pref.	Marg.	Pref.	Marg.	Pref.
Acq	Any acquisition					26	34					11	18
16R	Plans/programs					8	10	7	14	38	69	10	15
APE	Aerospace power employment					7	9	9	16			7	10
IO	Information operations					3	3	12	22			7	9
E&T	Education and training					6	8	6	13			5	8
21MYA	Munitions and missile maintenance, missile					10	12					4	6
33S	Communications and information systems			100	100	1	2	2	4			4	6
13SYC	Missile					8	10					3	5
16F	Foreign area							7	14			3	5
13S	Space or missile							6	13			3	4
16P	International political-military affairs					6	8	.1	.2			3	4
63A	Acquisition management					3	3					1	2
36P/38M	Personnel or manpower							1	3			.5	.8
RQ	Requirements					1	1					.5	.8
14N	Intelligence					.2	.3					.1	.1
Minimum with paired skill		0	0	100	100	79	100	50	100	38	69	62	93

employment) was the second largest, 16R (plans/programs) and 16F (foreign area specialist) tied for third, etc.[4]

The nonrated operations category needed relatively more new colonels with paired skills because the needs were high for its predominant career fields: 13S and 14N.

Table 5.3's columns for new 13S (space and missile) colonels raised some questions—for example, whether the needs differed much between space and missile officers and why some new colonels needed a paired skill in 13SYC (missile operations). As we noted above, about 40 percent of the new 13S colonels could come from more than one shredout. Table 5.4 shows how the balancing mechanism recommended that the flexible and other floors be coordinated across the 13S shredouts. It seemed natural that only 13SYCs (missileers) needed a paired skill in 21MYA (missile maintenance), and, of course, only nonmissileers (primarily those in 13SYB [space lift]) needed a paired skill in missiles. The most commonly recommended paired skill was Acq (acquisition), more frequently for space than for missile officers.[5] New missile colonels

Table 5.4
Balanced Percentage Floors for the Space and Missile Operations Development Team

		13SYA		13SYB		13SYC		13SYC		13SYE			
		Satellite C2		Space Lift		Missile Operations		Surveillance		Warning		All 13S Combined	
Paired Skill		Marg.	Pref.	Marg.	Pref.	Marg.	Pref.	Marg.	Pref.	Marg.	Pref.	Marg.	Pref.
Acq	Any acquisition	38	47	33	42	20	26	40	47	30	40	30	39
21MYA	Munitions and missile maintenance, missile					27	40					10	12
16R	Plans/programs	8	11	10	9	6	10	9	11	8	12	8	10
13SYC	Missile	5	3	24	26				3	8	11	8	10
APE	Aerospace power employment	10	12	9	10	1	2	10	12	7	10	7	9
E&T	Education and training	6	9	6	6	5	10	9	9	6	9	6	8
16P	International political-military affairs	6	9	4	5	6	9	9	9	6	9	6	8
IO	Information operations	4	4	3	1	2	4	4	4	3	4	3	3
33S	Communications and information systems	3	4	2	1			1	3	1	3	1	2
14N	Intelligence	.9	.7	.1				.0	.8	.2	2	.2	.3
Minimum with paired skill		81	100	91	100	67	100	82	100	68	100	79	100

[4] These paired skills are consistent with areas of experience that a subsequent study of the 14N career field found to be needed at grades O-4, O-5, and O-6 (Brauner et al., 2009).

[5] Table 5.4's totals for Acq reflect the sums of three rows in Table 5.3: Acq + 63A + RQ.

apparently needed APE less frequently than did new space colonels, and new missile colonels needed neither 33S (communications and information systems) nor 14N (intelligence) as paired skills. As noted previously, the preferred solution recommended that all new 13S colonels have a paired skill.[6]

Logistics Floors

Because the logistics career fields were in flux when this study's demand data were gathered, their floors emerged less clearly than those in other categories. Nevertheless, Table 5.5 displays results from applying the balancing mechanism, trying to distinguish the maintenance and logistics readiness subcategories. Note the oddities that at least 4 to 6 percent of the new maintenance colonels apparently needed a paired skill in maintenance and 5 to 17 percent of new colonels from logistics readiness needed a paired skill in 2YY (any logistics). Both result from the requirement data's partial distinction of more detailed requirements (e.g., for aircraft

Table 5.5
Balanced Percentage Floors for the Logistics Development Team

Paired skill		Maintenance		Logistics Readiness		Total	
		Marginal	Preferred	Marginal	Preferred	Marginal	Preferred
Acq	Any acquisition	10	16	8	15	9	16
21A/B/M	Maintenance	4	6	3	9	3	7
33S	Communications and information systems	5	7			2	5
2YY	Any logistics			5	17	2	5
E&T	Education and training	4	6			2	4
86M/86P	Operations management or command and control	2	3	2	7	2	4
16R	Plans/programs	2	.1	2	14	2	4
32E	Civil engineering	3	5			2	4
13S	Space or missile	3	5			2	4
21R	Logistics readiness	2	2			.8	2
Acq/21M	Any acquisition or equipment maintenance			4		2	
65F	Financial management			.6	2	.3	1
16P	International political-military affairs			.5	2	.2	.5
Minimum with paired skill		36	51	23	66	29	56

[6] Another reason that we include Table 5.4 was the Air Force's "Space Professional Program" (Space Professional Development, 2006), which tracked officers' growing range and depth of experience and facilitated more nuanced management and development than most other career fields. In spite of the differentiation that is possible within the career field, it still sought more integration and less differentiation between its previously distinct populations of space versus missile officers. Nevertheless, as Table 5.4 illustrates, meaningful differences naturally persisted.

maintenance versus equipment maintenance versus munitions and missile maintenance, and, on the logistics readiness side, for logistics plans versus supply versus transportation). We believed that the logistics development team should choose judiciously any elements of guidance in Table 5.5 that seemed reasonable and alter others as necessary. We recommended gathering fresh information about the positions' requirements in consistent terms and reapplying flow analysis, accounting insofar as possible for the interplay with nonlogistics career fields, and deriving better floors. In the meantime, we thought this work's prioritizations probably still could be useful: acquisition (a little more for maintenance officers), maintenance (for logistics readiness officers), 33S (communications and information systems) for maintenance officers, 16R (plans/programs), especially for logistics readiness officers), and perhaps E&T (education and training) for maintenance officers and 86M/86P (operations management or command and control) for both maintenance and logistics readiness officers.

Support and OSI Floors

Balancing was unnecessary for the support and OSI career fields because the flow analysis recommended just one career field for all of their entrants. Table 5.6 contains nearly the same information as Chapter Four's Table 4.6. These career fields' needs for paired skills were more modest than the needs in other categories. The needs in 35P (public affairs) were greatest, for 16P (political-military affairs) and 16R (plans/programs), next in 37F, comprising 36P and 38M (personnel and manpower) when the requirements data were gathered, and third in 33S (communications and information systems), primarily for information operations (IO) and political and military affairs (16P).

Floors for Acquisition and Finance

Finally, Table 5.7 lists the floors derived using the balancing method for new acquisition and finance colonels. The results were considerably less uniform than those for new rated colonels. For example:

- Only new 61S (scientist) and 62E (developmental engineering) colonels needed a paired skill specifically in 63A (acquisition management).
- Only new 61S (scientist) colonels needed a paired skill in generic 13S (space or missile operations).
- Only new 63A (acquisition management) colonels needed a paired skill in 62E (developmental engineering) or specifically in logistics (2YY, 21A/B/M, and 21R).
- Virtually only new 65X (finance) colonels needed a paired skills in MO (mobility operations) or flexibly in either 13SYC/21M (missile operations or munitions and missile maintenance).

Although not shown in Table 5.7, entrants shifted notably from 63A (acquisition management) to 65X (financial management) between the marginal and the preferred solutions' allocations. Moreover, although 63A provided the majority of the space paired skills in the marginal solution's allocation, the majority shifted to 64P (contracting) in the preferred solution's allocation.

Table 5.6
Percentage Floors for the Support and OSI Development Teams

		31P Security Forces		32E Civil Engineering		33S Communications and Information Systems		34M Services		35P Public Affairs		37F Personnel and Manpower		71S Special Investigation		All Support and OSI	
Paired skill		Marg.	Pref.	Marg.	Pref.	Marg.	Pref.	Marg.	Pref.	Marg.	Pref.	Marg.	Pref.	Marg.	Pref.	Marg.	Pref.
16R	Plans/programs			7	10					28	35	5	15			4	7
16P	International political-military affairs					4	12			42	51	1	2			4	7
IO	Information operations					10	11									3	3
36P	Personnel					4	11					2	7			2	4
13S	Space or missile											6	17			2	3
33S	Communications and information systems											6	17			2	3
21T/34M/ E&T	Transportation, services, or education and training	17	21													1	3
61S	Scientist											5	15			1	3
E&T	Education and training											2	7			.7	1.3
31P	Security forces													11	11	.5	1.0
APE	Aerospace power employment											2	5			.5	.9
14N	Intelligence					.8										.3	
13SYA/ B/D/E	Any space					.1	.1									.0	.0
Minimum with paired skill		17	21	7	10	19	34	.0	.0	71	86	29	86	11	11	21	36

Table 5.7
Balanced Percentage Floors for Acquisition and Finance Development Teams

		61S Scientist		62E Develop-mental Engineering		63A Acquisition Manage-ment		64P Contracting		65X Finance		All Acquisition/ Financial Combined	
Paired Skill		Marg.	Pref.	Marg.	Pref.	Marg.	Pref.	Marg.	Pref.	Marg.	Pref.	Marg.	Pref.
63A	Acquisition management	20	32	12	20							3	7
Acq	Any acquisition			10	24	.3				9	10	3	6
13SYA	Space satellite c2		4	2	5	4		5	15			3	5
13SYB	Space lift		4	2	5	4		5	16			3	5
36P	Personnel	15	19					7	6			2	4
16P/16R	Plan/programs or international political-military affairs					4	20					2	4
IO	Information operations	18	23			.5	3					2	4
MO	Mobility operations							1		9	12	2	3
62E	Developmental engineering					3	17					2	3
2YY	Any logistics					3	16					1	3
13SYC/21M	Missile or munitions and missile maint							1		9	10	1	3
13S	Space or missile	15	19									1	3
13SYE	Space warning							12	11			1	3
13SYD	Space surveillance			.2	1	2		3	10			1	3
13B/D/M	C2ISR					2	11					1	2
61S/62E	Scientist or developmental engineering					2	9					1	2
13B	Air battle manager					1	6					.7	1
13SYB/C	Space lift or missile			4	9							.6	1
33Y	Communications and information systems					1	5					.6	1
65F	Financial management					1	5					.6	1

Table 5.7—Continued

Paired Skill		61S Scientist Marg.	61S Scientist Pref.	62E Developmental Engineering Marg.	62E Developmental Engineering Pref.	63A Acquisition Management Marg.	63A Acquisition Management Pref.	64P Contracting Marg.	64P Contracting Pref.	65X Finance Marg.	65X Finance Pref.	All Acquisition/ Financial Combined Marg.	All Acquisition/ Financial Combined Pref.
16R/21R/ 33S	Plans/programs, logistics readiness, or communicaitons/ information									2	3	.3	.8
16R	Plans/programs									3	2	.5	.6
13SYA/B/ D/E	Any space					.5	3					.3	.5
21A/B/M	Maintenance					.5	3					.2	.5
21R	Logistics readiness					.3	2					.2	.3
SA	Safety									.9	1	.1	.3
APE	Aerospace power employment					.3	1					.1	.3
13S/14N	Space, missile, or intelligence			5	2							.8	.2
64P	Contracting					.1	.5					.1	.1
Minimum with paired skill		68	100	35	66	31	100	35	58	33	38	36	67

Final Adjustments

AFPC adjusted some of the percentages in Tables 5.2–5.3 and 5.5–5.7 before promulgating them. Appendix E displays the briefing slides that AF/DPP and AFPC used when they first presented the new floors to CFMs and DTs in early FY 2006. Adjustments include the following:

- CAF: merged Table 5.2's paired skill 2YY/63A (any logistics or acquisition management) into 6YY (acquisition or finance).
- MAF: merged Table 5.2's paired skills 2YY/63A (any logistics or acquisition management) into 6YY (acquisition or finance) and omitted EW (electronic warfare).
- SOF: merged into 21X (any logistics) Table 5.2's paired skills 2YY/63A (any logistics or acquisition management) and 21R (logistics readiness).
- 13M: displayed Table 5.2's equal floors of 100 percent with paired skill 33S (communications and information systems) as 99 percent to 100 percent.
- 13S: merged with Acq (any acquisition) Table 5.3's paired skills 63A (acquisition management) and RQ (requirements).
- 37F: omitted Table 5.5's 36P (personnel), a residual from the previous split between the 36P (personnel) and 38M (manpower) AFSCs.
- 61S: merged into 13S (space) Table 5.6's 13S (space or missile), 13SYA (space satellite command and control), and 13SYB (space lift).

- 62E: merged into 13S (space or missile) Table 5.6's 13SYA (space satellite command and control), 13SYB (space lift), 13SYD (space surveillance), 13SYB/C (space lift or missile), and 13S/14N (space, missile, or intelligence).
- 63A: merged into 21X (any logistics) Table 5.6's 2YY (any logistics), 21A/B/M (maintenance), and 21R (logistics readiness), and merged into 13S (space) Table 5.6's 13SYA (space satellite command and control), 13SYB (space lift), 13SYD (space surveillance), and 13SYA/B/D/E (any space).
- 64P: merged into 13S (space or missile) Table 5.6's 13SYA (space satellite command and control), 13SYB (space lift), 13SYC/21M (missile or munitions and missile maintenance), 13SYE (space warning), and 13SYD (space surveillance).
- 65X: relabeled 16R/21R/33S (plans/programs, logistics readiness, or communications and information systems) as 21R or 33Y (logistics readiness or communications/informations) and omitted SA (safety).

Slides 9–12 in Appendix E use the MAF to illustrate steps for applying skill-pairing floors, establishing minimum numbers of officers in one or more cohorts who should be vectored into various paired skills:

- Slide 9 applies the floor percentages to the 1990 cohort of 314 MAF officers—for example, targeting at least 15 and preferably at least 39 officers vectored into 16R (plans/programs).
- Slide 10 depicts the floor percentages used in Slide 9.
- Slide 11 breaks the numbers calculated in Slide 9 into segments reflecting that, for the plans/programs paired skill, for example:
  - Four MAF officers already had developed it.
  - One had been vectored but had not yet developed it.
  - Ten more needed vectoring into the paired skill to reach 15, corresponding to the marginal percentage floor for new colonels
  - Twenty-four beyond that needed vectoring to reach 39, corresponding to the preferred percentage floor.
- Slide 12 shows related counts that combine the 1984 to 1986 cohorts—that is, the three cohorts with four to six years more experience than the 1990 cohort. For the (16R) (plans/programs) paired skill, for example, about 97 officers already had developed the skill, exceeding the 83 corresponding to the (preferred) percentage floor. Apparently, about eight officers already had developed a paired skill in IO (information operations), enough to match the marginal floor's percentage but three short of matching the preferred floor's percentage.
- Slide 12 makes the important point that, although generally enough officers in the 1984 to 1986 MAF cohorts already had the targeted paired skills, it is important that enough suitably developed officers actually get promoted to colonel. If too few officers of the caliber the Air Force promotes to colonel develop the targeted paired skills, then some of the colonels and generals eventually selected from those cohorts will sometimes be harder to place (because their skills will not match enough positions' requirements), will have more difficulty performing some jobs at those grades (when they are assigned without the paired skill to a position that needs it), or will need to develop a paired skill after promotion to colonel.

Clearly, the floors' graphic representations, their straightforward applicability to year groups (and to collections of year groups), and the simple comparisons they allow could readily help development teams assess how many officers, if any, either (1) have already developed the necessary paired skills, (2) have been vectored into the necessary paired skills but have not developed them yet, or (3) still need to be vectored to meet specified minimums. At least for purposes of sustaining a well-configured force of colonels, many majors and lieutenant colonels need not be vectored into paired skills at all, even if they, their career fields, or the Air Force might benefit for other reasons. Beyond guiding enough officers in total into the necessary paired skills, development teams would need to work to ensure that enough officers with high potential for being promoted to colonel develop those skills.

CHAPTER SIX

Conclusions

Here, we recommend ways to improve the skill-pairing floors and summarize this work's thematic lessons.

Ways to Improve the Skill-Pairing Floors

Before disseminating new targets to the development teams, AF/A1 assembled a working group[1] of CFMs to assess whether they seemed reasonable, aiming to avoid a negative reception such as the one that met AFPC's wide promulgation during 2004 of AFSLMO's guidance about developmental assignments. The working group judged the floors generally reasonable and sufficiently justified, recommending that development teams adjust them as necessary if they disagreed with the experts' characterizations of some positions' requirements or if they needed to reflect changes since 2002 or changes anticipated in the future.[2] It would be informative to identify and summarize whether and how development teams may have adjusted the floors identified in this report, in the process gathering insights about improvements that may be possible in both the data and methodology. Even without conducting such a review and assessment, the following steps would strengthen the occupational developmental floors:

- Update and forecast colonel positions' requirements for occupational skills, and experience as colonels, plus the sets of jobs that should be reserved largely for fast-track, high-potential officers. We recommend special effort to estimate *future* requirements, reflecting at least the degree to which the overall types and mixes of primary and paired skills are likely to change.[3] This would help enable the identification of pre-colonel developmental programs that would be robust across a range of possible future requirements.

---

1 This report's acknowledgments list the working group's members.

2 The working group also observed that many career fields already provide numerous officers with experience in the targeted paired skills. For example, many rated officers gain experience in APE (aerospace power employment), Acq (acquisition), or 16R (plans/programs) without being assigned outside of their AFSCs.

3 The incumbent survey that AFSLMO began during 2005 but never completed had those goals, along with obtaining important additional information about positions' requirements and identifying requirements for civilian GS-15 positions. The survey also addressed the medical, legal, and clergy professions. It could be revisited, revitalized, and refielded. A workshop method, similar to the one described in Chapter Two, also could be considered.

- Similarly, update and forecast the GO inflow requirements. To what degree have they changed and how are they likely to change in the future?[4] An identified variety of possible future requirements could feed into this report's analytic framework and help ensure that correspondingly revised pre-colonel developmental floors would be suitably robust.
- Identify the skill requirements for GS-15 positions and assess O-6 and GS-15 flows and alignments in an integrated manner, paralleling the approach for the top-level force of GOs and SES members. Shifts are likely to be possible between the O-6 and GS-15 forces that could simultaneously strengthen operational and functional management and facilitate the creation and sustainment of practical progression and experience profiles for both officers and civilians.
- Reflect learning in the models of flows and position/inventory alignments (from O-6 through O-10 and corresponding civilian grades)—that is, assess the degree to which individuals may gain important skills during these grades. The more this is possible, the less development is necessary at lower grades. Other research has demonstrated modeling methods that reflect learning.[5]
- Reflect uncertainties, especially about the retention of enough individuals with specific combinations of skills. The smaller the pyramid of colonels with a particular combination of skills, the greater the uncertainty about whether enough properly qualified individuals will be available when openings occur. Taking this into account would further limit occupational flexibility. Other sources of uncertainty include promotion selection and the times spent in positions and grades.
- Refine estimates of behavioral parameters—that is, retention rates and job durations. Look for differences across occupational groups—for example, rated versus nonrated colonels—as well as between fast-trackers and others.
- Address inventory and flow floors in greater detail—that is, more along the lines of Tables 4.3–4.7 than Tables 5.2, 5.3, and 5.5–5.7. This could lead some DTs to consider finer gradations within their career fields—for example, the rated DTs might adopt different but coordinated goals for officers from different weapon systems (fighters versus bombers versus C2ISR for the CAF team, say), or today's force-support team (for Air Force Speciality [AFS] 38F, which merged the previous 34M, 36P, 37F, and 38M) might adopt somewhat different goals for its major functional areas (manpower, personnel, education/training, services, for example).
- Reflect past and future developmental opportunities—that is, track individuals' accumulation of experience in the various skill areas and the availability within and across career fields of positions that offer experience therein. This would help the Air Force assess the developmental health of cohorts within its officer career fields, enhance the utiliza-

[4] Several times since this report's work was completed, AF/DPG [the Air Force General Officer Management Office] and RAND have updated the database that delineates GO jobs' needs for occupational competencies and reassessed the occupational mix needed in incoming GOs. One thread in that work examined the potential effects on developmental needs if the future called for more GOs in information and space operations and opened to them more leadership jobs that traditionally have accepted only rated GOs.

[5] George Vernez, S. Craig Moore, Steven Martino, and Jeffrey Yuen, *Improving the Development and Utilization of Air Force Space and Missile Officers,* Santa Monica, Calif.: RAND Corporation, MG-382-AF, 2006; Henry A. Leonard, J. Michael Polich, Jeffrey D. Peterson, Ronald E. Sortor, and S. Craig Moore, *Something Old, Something New: Army Leader Development in a Dynamic Environment,* Santa Monica, Calif.: RAND Corporation, MG-281-A, 2006.

tion of experience already gained, minimize additional officer assignments specifically to gain certain skills, and perhaps largely eliminate the need to balance the development of paired skills using an allocation method such as that in Chapter Five.

Thematic Lessons

This research reconfirmed that multiple skills are needed for many leadership positions, although for a smaller fraction of O-6 positions than of GO positions. It also found, as we have seen in other contexts, that groups of jobs that call for particular skills often do not have pyramid-shaped experience profiles—for example, more positions may need officers who have held a previous O-6 job than not. Together, these needs imply that more colonels than jobs need multiple skills. Ensuring selectivity—that is, multiple qualified candidates available for selection and assignment per opening—increases the differences even further.

Flow analysis that reflects jobs' needs for experience, primary skills, and paired skills; that reserves most so-called platform jobs for colonels expected to be competitive for promotion to GO; that takes into account the needs for occupational skills among the colonels eventually selected for GO; and that maintains pyramidal experience profiles for inventories of colonels can help establish the minimum numbers of new colonels who should have each skill combination. The minimums can differ dramatically from those calculated via common fair-sharing methods, and they vary with policy parameters. For example, the more selectivity desired and the closer that colonels' prior experience and promotion potential must match their positions' designations, the less flexible becomes the recommended mix of primary occupations among new colonels and the more new colonels are recommended with paired skills. Although Air Force experts judged that only about 22 percent of approximately 2,800 line O-6 positions in 2002 needed paired skills, flow analysis recommended that at least 31 percent and preferably at least 58 percent of the average cohort of new colonels have paired skills. Although still higher percentages would be acceptable for purposes of personnel management, of course, they are unnecessary and could reduce valuable depth of experience in primary skills for colonels who will not need the breadth.

The operational and support communities' experts judged that many O-6 jobs could or should be open to a wider range of occupations than the USAF's authorizations indicated. That is, many jobs' actual primary occupational requirements were more flexible than authorized. For example, the experts marked only 15 (12 percent) of the 126 O-6 jobs authorized for 11F (fighter pilot) as actually needing fighter pilots specifically, and only 70 (37 percent) of the 190 authorized for 63A (acquisition manager) as needing acquisition managers specifically. Their more flexible designations let our flow analysis recommend inflows and corresponding inventories of colonels who could fulfill all jobs' needs for primary or paired occupational skills and most of their needs for experience and selectivity. The closer the fulfillment of jobs' designated needs for experience and selectivity, and, for platform jobs, the need for colonels with better prospects of promotion to GO, the more new colonels who should bring paired skills.

Fortunately, most of the paired skills needed seem already to be available to officers from the appropriate primary occupations. Many O-4 and O-5 jobs at the Air Staff and MAJCOM headquarters provide experience in planning and programming, many in numbered air forces and joint combatant commands provide backgrounds in aerospace power employment, and so on. The key seems to be for the Air Force to identify and deliberately channel through such jobs enough of each career field's officers who have high potential for eventually making colonel.

This research concentrated on the mixes of paired skills that officers from different specialties should develop before they become colonels, but it also illuminated the mix of primary occupations needed in the colonel force. The analysis recommended that rated officers constitute about 34 to 41 percent of the total (down from the 47 percent seen in 2005's actual force), that logistics officers constitute about 12 to 14 percent (up from 2005's actual 10 percent), and that acquisition/finance constitute about 18 percent (up from 2005's actual 13 percent). Noteworthy shifts at a more detailed level (so-called core [three-character] AFSCs) included recommendations that control and recovery (13D) represent about 3 to 5 percent of the nonrated operations total (up from 2005's 2 percent), that public affairs (35P) represent about 4 to 7 percent of the support and OSI total (up from 2005's 3 percent), that scientist (61S) represent about 9 to 13 percent of the acquisition/finance total (up from 2005's 8 percent), and that developmental engineering (62E) represent about 8 to 12 percent of the acquisition/finance total (down from 2005's 29 percent). Because preserving 2005's mix of primary occupations was among the goals in this analysis, the optimizations recommended such shifts to improve the O-6 force on measures accorded higher priorities—that is, matching candidates' backgrounds with the O-6 jobs' occupational needs, providing selectivity (multiple suitable candidates per opening), some jobs' designations for high-potential officers or needs for prior O-6 experience, and pools of senior colonels with the skills needed in the incoming GO force. This research did not try to assess how much those other objectives would be compromised if the Air Force wanted to maintain more nearly the mix of primary occupations seen in 2005's colonels.

APPENDIX A

Line Colonel Positions' Requirements for Experience and Occupational Skills

This appendix lists the numbers of FY 2002's authorized O-6 positions that the Air Force experts said needed each primary occupational skill, each secondary or paired occupational skill, and each experience level. Although the positions were also categorized as either platform positions (appropriate for fast-track colonels) or not, that distinction is not displayed here because the information was considered sensitive.

Please note that each officer specialty was acceptable for more than one primary skill group. For example, 11Bs (bomber pilots) were acceptable in positions designated for any of the following 27 primary skills or alternatives:

11B (bomber pilot)

11B/12B (bomber)

11F/11B (fighter or bomber pilot)

11Y (pilot)

FB (fighter or bomber)

FB/13B (fighter, bomber, or ABM)

FB/1YM (fighter, bomber, or mobility)

RT not 13B (any rated except ABM)

RT (rated)

11B/12B/13SYC (bomber or missile)

11B/12B/3YY (bomber or any support)

1YY (any operations)

1YY/33Y/62E (any operations, communications/information systems, or developmental engineering)

1YY/62EYF (any operations or flight test developmental engineering)

1YY/63A (any operations or acquisition management)

1YY/65F/65W (any operations, financial management, or cost analysis)

1YY/65Y (any operations or finance)

FBA/63A (fighter, bomber, airlift, or acquisition management)

RT/13M (any rated or airfield operations)

RT/13S (any rated, space, or missile)

RT/13Y (any rated, space, missile, or C2)

RT/13Y/14N (any rated, space, missile, C2, or intelligence)

RT/14N (any rated or intelligence)

RT/21G (any rated or logistics plans)

RT/21M (any rated or munitions and missile maintenance)

RT/2YY (any rated or any logistics)

any (any)

Table A.1
Number of Jobs Requiring Different Occupational Skills and Levels of Experience

						Required Experience Level(s)						
Required Primary Skill Category	Required Primary Skill Code	Required Primary Skill	Required Secondary Skill Category	Required Secondary Skill Code	Required Secondary Skill	Any	1st Job	1st or 2nd	2nd Job	2nd or Senior	Senior Job	Total
Rated	11A	Airlift pilot	None	None	None	1	11		3		5	20
	11A/12A	Airlift	None	None	None		8	3	5		1	17
	11B	Bomber pilot	Acquisition and finance	6YY	Acquisition/financial management						1	1
	11B/12B	Bomber	None	None	None	1	1		4		4	10
			Other	Acq/2YY	Any acquisition or any logistics	1						1
	11E	Experimental-test pilot	Acquisition and finance	62EYF	Flight test developmental engineering		1					1
	11F	Fighter pilot	None	None	None	4	3	8	42	4	16	77
			Family of operations	APE	Aerospace power employment				1		1	2
			Nonrated operations	16R	Plans/programs				2			2
			Acquisition and finance	Acq	Any acquisition	3			1			4
	11F/11B	Fighter or bomber pilot	None	None	None				1			1
	11F/11H	Fighter or helicopter pilot	None	None	None	1			1			2
	11H	Helicopter pilot	None	None	None			1	1			2
	11H/11S/12S	Helicopter pilot or SOF	None	None	None	1	2	2	7	2	2	16
			Nonrated operations	16R	Plans/programs				1		1	2
	11M	Mobility pilot	None	None	None	1	5		2		1	9
	11R	Reconnaissance pilot	None	None	None				1			1
	11S/12S	Special operations (SOF)	None	None	None	4		1	7		5	17
			Nonrated operations	16R	Plans/programs			1				1
			Acquisition and finance	6YY	Acquisition/financial management				1			1

Table A.1—Continued

Required Primary Skill Category	Required Primary Skill Code	Required Primary Skill	Required Secondary Skill Category	Required Secondary Skill Code	Required Secondary Skill	Required Experience Level(s)						
						Any	1st Job	1st or 2nd	2nd Job	2nd or Senior	Senior Job	Total
	11Y	Pilot	None	None	None			19	10	6	5	40
			Support and OSI	36P/38M	Personnel or manpower	1						1
			Other	2YY/63A	Any logistics or acquisition management				1			1
	13A	Astronaut	None	None	None		8		1			9
	13B	Air battle manager	None	None	None	2			2			4
	1YE	Experimental-test	None	None	None				1			1
			Acquisition and finance	6YY	Acquisition/financial management		2	1	1		3	7
	1YF	Fighter	None	None	None	1	3	3	4		5	16
			Family of operations	APE	Aerospace power employment				1			1
			Nonrated operations	16R	Plans/programs	1						1
			Acquisition and finance	Acq	Any acquisition	1			1			2
	1YF/13B	Fighter or ABM	None	None	None	2					2	4
	1YF/1YM	Fighter or mobility	None	None	None				1			1
	1YM	Mobility	None	None	None	32	13	1	13		7	66
			Family of operations	MO	Mobility operations				1			1
			Nonrated operations	16R	Plans/programs	4			5			9
			Acquisition and finance	63A	Acquisition management	1						1
				Acq	Any acquisition	2			2			4
	1YM/11S/12S	Mobility or SOF	None	None	None	1						1
	1YR	Reconnaissance	None	None	None				1			1
			Acquisition and finance	Acq	Any acquisition	2						2
	1YR/13B	Reconnaissance or ABM	None	None	None				2		2	4
	1YT	Tanker	None	None	None		7		2		8	17

Table A.1—Continiued

Required Primary Skill Category	Required Primary Skill Code	Required Primary Skill	Required Secondary Skill Category	Required Secondary Skill Code	Required Secondary Skill	Required Experience Level(s): Any	1st Job	1st or 2nd	2nd Job	2nd or Senior	Senior Job	Total
	FB	Fighter or bomber	None	None	None	11			10		2	23
			Family of operations	APE	Aerospace power employment	10			2			12
				IO	Information operations	1						1
			Acquisition and finance	Acq	Any acquisition	7			5		1	13
			Other	Acq/2YY	Any acquisition or any logistics	2						2
	FB/13B	Fighter, Bomber, or ABM	None	None	None				1		2	3
	FB/1YM	Fighter, bomber, or mobility	None	None	None	1					1	2
			Family of operations	APE	Aerospace power employment			1	1			2
	FB/1YM/ 11S/ 12S	Fighter, bomber, mobility, or SOF	None	None	None				1			1
	FBA	Fighter, bomber, or airlift	None	None	None	9	10	2	15		2	38
			Nonrated operations	16R	Plans/programs				1			1
			Acquisition and finance	Acq	Any acquisition	1						1
	RT	Any rated	None	None	None	42	9	3	43	2	22	121
			Family of operations	APE	Aerospace power employment	13			4		4	21
				EW	Electronic warfare				1			1
				IO	Information operations	2	1		1			4
				MO	Mobility operations		1					1
			Nonrated operations	14N	Intelligence						1	1
				16F/16P	Foreign area or international political-military affairs	1						1
				16R	Plans/programs	8	2		6	3	4	23

Table A.1—Continued

Required Primary Skill Category	Required Primary Skill Code	Required Primary Skill	Required Secondary Skill Category	Required Secondary Skill Code	Required Secondary Skill	Required Experience Level(s): Any	1st Job	1st or 2nd	2nd Job	2nd or Senior	Senior Job	Total
			Support and OSI	36P/38M	Personnel or manpower						1	1
			Acquisition and finance	6YY	Acquisition/financial management	1					1	2
				Acq	Any acquisition	2	3		4			9
	RT not 13B	Any rated except ABM	None	None	None			7	13	3	6	29
			Support and OSI	36P/38M	Personnel or manpower				1			1
			Acquisition and finance	62E/63A	Developmental engineering or acquisition management				1			1
				6YY	Acquisition/financial management	1		1		2	1	5
Rated total						179	90	54	239	22	117	701
Nonrated operations	13D	Control and recovery	None	None	None				1			1
	13M	Airfield operations	Support and OSI	33Y	Communications and information systems		1					1
	13S	Space or missile	None	None	None	12	2		6			20
			Family of operations	APE	Aerospace power employment				1			1
				IO	Information operations	2						2
			Nonrated operations	16P	International political-military affairs	4	1					5
				16R	Plans/programs	1	3		3			7
			Logistics	21MYA	Munitions and missile maintenance, missile		1					1
			Acquisition and finance	Acq	Any acquisition	1	2		3			6
			Other	E&T	Education and training		1	1				2
	13S/14N	Space, missile, or intelligence	None	None	None	2	2	1			1	6

Table A.1—Continued

Required Primary Skill Category	Required Primary Skill Code	Required Primary Skill	Required Secondary Skill Category	Required Secondary Skill Code	Required Secondary Skill	Required Experience Level(s): Any	1st Job	1st or 2nd	2nd Job	2nd or Senior	Senior Job	Total
			Family of operations	IO	Information operations		1					1
	13SYA	Space satellite C2	Acquisition and finance	Acq	Any acquisition		1				3	4
	13SYA/B/D/E	Any space	None	None	None		1					1
			Family of operations	APE	Aerospace power employment		1					1
			Acquisition and finance	Acq	Any acquisition		1					1
	13SYA/D/E	Space satellite C2, surveillance, or warning	None	None	None				1			1
	13SYB	Space lift	Nonrated operations	13SYC	Missile		2					2
				16R	Plans/programs	1						1
			Acquisition and finance	Acq	Any acquisition		3				2	5
	13SYC	Missile	None	None	None	1	4		1			6
			Logistics	21M	Munitions and missile maintenance		1					1
				21MYA	Munitions and missile maintenance, missile		1		1		9	11
			Acquisition and finance	Acq	Any acquisition		1					1
			Other	Acq/2YY	Any acquisition or any logistics		1					1
	13SYD	Space surveillance	None	None	None		1					1
			Acquisition and finance	Acq	Any acquisition		1					1
	13SYD/E	Space surveillance or space warning	Acquisition and finance	Acq	Any acquisition		1				1	2
	13Y	Space, missile, or C2	Family of operations	APE	Aerospace power employment		1					1
	14N	Intelligence	None	None	None	15	8	5	12	7	3	50
			Family of operations	APE	Aerospace power employment	5			2	1	1	9

Table A.1—Continued

Required Primary Skill Category	Required Primary Skill Code	Required Primary Skill	Required Secondary Skill Category	Required Secondary Skill Code	Required Secondary Skill	Required Experience Level(s): Any	1st Job	1st or 2nd	2nd Job	2nd or Senior	Senior Job	Total
				APE/IO	Aerospace power employment or information operations						2	2
				IO	Information operations	1	5		6		3	15
			Nonrated operations	13S	Space or missile		1					1
				16F	Foreign area				1			1
				16F/16P	Foreign area or international political-military affairs				1			1
				16R	Plans/programs	1						1
			Other	E&T	Education and training			1				1
	15W	Weather	None	None	None	7	1		1	1	3	13
			Nonrated operations	16R	Plans/programs		2					2
Nonrated operations total						53	52	8	40	9	28	190
Logistics	21A	Aircraft maintenance	None	None	None		1	1	1			3
	21B	Equipment maintenance	None	None	None	10	32	15	46	1	7	111
			Nonrated operations	13S	Space or missile						1	1
			Logistics	21M	Munitions and missile maintenance				1			1
			Support and OSI	32E	Civil engineering			1				1
			Acquisition and finance	63A	Acquisition management				2			2
				6YY	Acquisition/financial management						1	1
			Other	Acq/2YY	Any acquisition or any logistics	3						3
				E&T	Education and training			2				2

Table A.1—Continued

Required Primary Skill Category	Required Primary Skill Code	Required Primary Skill	Required Secondary Skill Category	Required Secondary Skill Code	Required Secondary Skill	Required Experience Level(s)						
						Any	1st Job	1st or 2nd	2nd Job	2nd or Senior	Senior Job	Total
	21B/21R	Equipment maintenance or logistics readiness	None	None	None	6	6	1	9		5	27
			Acquisition and finance	63A	Acquisition management				1			1
				6YY	Acquisition/financial management				1			1
			Other	Acq/2YY	Any acquisition or any logistics	4						4
	21G	Logistics plans	None	None	None	2	1				1	4
			Logistics	2YY	Any logistics	1			2			3
			Other	Acq/21M	Any acquisition or munitions and missile maintenance		1					1
				Any	Any				1			1
	21M	Munitions and missile maintenance	Acquisition and finance	63A	Acquisition management				2			2
	21MYA	Munitions and missile maintenance, missile	None	None	None		4		4			8
	21MYB	Munitions and missile maintenance, spacelift	None	None	None				1			1
			Support and OSI	33Y	Communications and information systems		3					3
	21R	Logistics readiness	None	None	None	18	16	4	26	3	3	70
	21S	Supply	None	None	None				1			1
	21T	Transportation	None	None	None				1			1
	2YY	Any logistics	None	None	None		1	1	1			3
			Nonrated operations	16R	Plans/programs				1			1
Logistics total						44	65	25	101	4	18	257

Table A.1—Continued

Required Primary Skill Category	Required Primary Skill Code	Required Primary Skill	Required Secondary Skill Category	Required Secondary Skill Code	Required Secondary Skill	Required Experience Level(s)						
						Any	1st Job	1st or 2nd	2nd Job	2nd or Senior	Senior Job	Total
Support and OSI	31P	Security forces	None	None	None	8	2	2	21	3	3	39
			Other	21T/34M/ E&T	Transportation, services, or education/training			1				1
	31P/36P	Security forces or personnel	None	None	None			1				1
	32E	Civil engineering	None	None	None	9	17	1	36		11	74
	32E/34M	Civil engineering or services	None	None	None	1						1
	33Y	Communications and information systems	None	None	None	68	19	6	20	5	9	127
			Family of operations	IO	Information operations	1	1					2
			Support and OSI	36P	Personnel						1	1
	34M	Services	None	None	None	6	2		3		8	19
	35B	Band	None	None	None	1						1
	35P	Public affairs	None	None	None	3			1			4
			Nonrated operations	16P	International political-military affairs	3	3		4	1		11
				16R	Plans/programs	5					1	6
	36P	Personnel	None	None	None	6	10		8	1	4	29
			Nonrated operations	13S	Space or missile				1			1
			Support and OSI	33Y	Communications and information systems		1		1			2
			Acquisition and finance	61S	Scientist						1	1
	36P/38M	Personnel or manpower	None	None	None	23	12	1	5	3	5	49
			Nonrated operations	16R	Plans/programs		1					1
	38M	Manpower	None	None	None	1	4	1	2		1	9
			Support and OSI	36P	Personnel					1		1
	3YY	Any support	None	None	None			1	3			4

Table A.1—Continued

Required Primary Skill Category	Required Primary Skill Code	Required Primary Skill	Required Secondary Skill Category	Required Secondary Skill Code	Required Secondary Skill	Required Experience Level(s): Any	1st Job	1st or 2nd	2nd Job	2nd or Senior	Senior Job	Total
			Other	Any	Any	1						1
				E&T	Education and training					1		1
	71S	Special investigations	None	None	None	7			13			20
Support and OSI total						143	72	14	118	15	44	406
Acquisition and finance	61S	Scientist	None	None	None	3			2		11	16
			Family of operations	IO	Information operations				1			1
			Nonrated operations	13S	Space or missile	1						1
			Support and OSI	36P	Personnel		1					1
			Acquisition and finance	63A	Acquisition management	1			1			2
	61S/62E	Scientist or developmental engineering	None	None	None		2		4		1	7
			Acquisition and finance	63A	Acquisition management		4		8	1		13
	61S/62E/63A	Scientist, developmental engineering, or acquisition management	None	None	None	2					1	3
			Acquisition and finance	63A	Acquisition management				1			1
	61SYA	Analytical scientist	Nonrated operations	13S	Space or missile		1					1
	62E	Developmental engineering	None	None	None	8	1	1	1	1	5	17
			Nonrated operations	13S/14N	Space, missile, or intelligence	3						3
				13SYB/C	Space lift or missile	1						1
			Acquisition and finance	Acq	Any acquisition		1					1
	62E/63A	Developmental engineering or acquisition management	None	None	None						1	1

Table A.1—Continued

Required Primary Skill Category	Required Primary Skill Code	Required Primary Skill	Required Secondary Skill Category	Required Secondary Skill Code	Required Secondary Skill	Required Experience Level(s)						Total
						Any	1st Job	1st or 2nd	2nd Job	2nd or Senior	Senior Job	
	63A	Acquisition management	None	None	None	8	12	1	16		8	45
			Rated	13B	Air battle manager	1						1
			Nonrated operations	13B/D/M	C2ISR				1			1
				16P/16R	Plan/programs or international political-military affairs				2			2
			Logistics	2YY	Any logistics				2			2
			Acquisition and finance	61S/62E	Scientist or developmental engineering	5	1		4		1	11
				62E	Developmental engineering		1		1			2
				65F	Financial management	1						1
				Acq	Any acquisition	1						1
			Other	13S/62E	Space, missile, or developmental engineering		1					1
	64P	Contracting	None	None	None	8	12	2	17		2	41
			Nonrated operations	13SYE	Space warning		1					1
			Support and OSI	36P	Personnel					2		2
	65F	Financial management	None	None	None	8	5	2	31	1	4	51
			Acquisition and finance	Acq	Any acquisition		1					1
			Other	16R/21R/33Y	Plans/programs, logistics readiness, or communications/information					1		1
	65F/65W	Financial management or cost analysis	None	None	None		1		1			2
	65W	Cost analysis	None	None	None		1					1

Table A.1—Continued

Required Primary Skill Category	Required Primary Skill Code	Required Primary Skill	Required Secondary Skill Category	Required Secondary Skill Code	Required Secondary Skill	Required Experience Level(s)						
						Any	1st Job	1st Or 2nd	2nd Job	2nd Or Senior	Senior Job	Total
	6YY	Acquisition/financial management	None	None	None	45	24		15		3	87
			Family of operations	MO	Mobility operations				1			1
			Nonrated operations	13S	Space or missile		2		6		1	9
				13S/14N	Space, missile, or intelligence					1		1
				13S/15W	Space, missile, or weather	1			1			2
			Support and OSI	33Y	Communications and information systems	1						1
			Other	13SYB/C/21M	Space lift, missile, or munitions and missile maintenance	1						1
				13SYC/21M	Missile or munitions and missile maintenance						1	1
				1YY	Any operations	1	1		2			4
				1YY/21A	Any operations or aircraft maintenance	1			5		1	7
				1YY/2YY	Any operations or any logistics				1			1
	Acq	Any acquisition	None	None	None	1	7		1		1	10
			Nonrated operations	13S	Space or missile				1			1
				13SYA	Space satellite c2		8				2	10
				13SYA/15W	Space satellite c2 or weather		1					1
				13SYA/B/D/E	Any space		1		1		2	4
				13SYA/E	Space satellite c2 or space warning		1				1	2
				13SYB	Space lift		7		1		1	9
				13SYB/C	Space lift or missile		1				1	2

Table A.1—Continued

Required Primary Skill Category	Required Primary Skill Code	Required Primary Skill	Required Secondary Skill Category	Required Secondary Skill Code	Required Secondary Skill	Required Experience Level(s): Any	1st Job	1st or 2nd	2nd Job	2nd or Senior	Senior Job	Total
				13SYD	Space surveillance		1					1
				13SYD/E	Space surveillance or space warning		3					3
				13SYE	Space warning		1					1
Acquisition and finance total						102	104	6	128	7	48	395
Other (more than one skill category)	11A/12A/63A	Airlift or acquisition management	None	None	None				1			1
	11B/12B/13SYC	Bomber or missile	None	None	None	7	3		4			14
			Nonrated operations	16R	Plans/programs	1						1
	11B/12B/3YY	Bomber or any support	None	None	None	2					1	3
	11S/12S/13D	SOF or control and recovery	None	None	None						1	1
	11S/12S/13DYA	SOF or control and recovery rescue	None	None	None	1	1					2
	11S/12S/13DYB	SOF or control and recovery special tactics	None	None	None						1	1
	13B/13D	ABM or control and recovery	None	None	None	1				1		2
	13B/13S/33Y/36P	ABM, space, missile, communications/information, or personnel	None	None	None			1				1
	13S/14N/61S/62E	Space, missile, intelligence, scientist, or developmental engineering	None	None	None			1				1
	13S/62E	Space, missile, or developmental engineering	None	None	None	3						3

Table A.1—Continued

Required Primary Skill Category	Required Primary Skill Code	Required Primary Skill	Required Secondary Skill Category	Required Secondary Skill Code	Required Secondary Skill	Required Experience Level(s): Any	1st Job	1st or 2nd	2nd Job	2nd or Senior	Senior Job	Total
	13S/63A	Space, missile, or acquisition management	Other	13S/63A	Space, missile, or acquisition management	1						1
	13S/6YY	Space, missile, or acquisition/financial management	None	None	None	4						4
	14N/33Y	Intelligence or communications/ information systems	Family of operations	IO	Information operations		1					1
			Nonrated operations	14N	Intelligence	1	1				1	3
			Other	14N/33Y	Intelligence or communications/ information systems	1						1
	1YM/21R	Mobility or logistics readiness	None	None	None		8					8
	1YR/13B/ 14N/33Y	Reconnaissance, air battle management, intelligence, or communications/ information	Nonrated operations	16R	Plans/programs	3		1	1			5
			Acquisition and finance	Acq	Any acquisition				1			1
			Other	Acq/2YY	Any acquisition or any logistics	2						2
	1YR/14N	Reconnaissance or intelligence	Acquisition and finance	63A	Acquisition management				1			1
				6YY	Acquisition/financial management					1		1
	1YY	Any operations	None	None	None	25	2	2	28	3	2	62
			Nonrated operations	14N	Intelligence	7		1	2		2	12
				16P	International political-military affairs	4			1		1	6
				16R	Plans/programs		2		5	1		8

Table A.1—Continued

Required Primary Skill Category	Required Primary Skill Code	Required Primary Skill	Required Secondary Skill Category	Required Secondary Skill Code	Required Secondary Skill	Required Experience Level(s): Any	1st Job	1st or 2nd	2nd Job	2nd or Senior	Senior Job	Total
			Support and OSI	33Y	Communications and information systems	2			3		1	6
			Acquisition and finance	63A	Acquisition management				1	1		2
				Acq	Any acquisition	8	1		1			10
	1YY/2YY	Any operations or any logistics	Acquisition and finance	63A	Acquisition management				1			1
	1YY/33Y	Any operations or communications/ information systems	Family of operations	IO	Information operations	1	9		2			12
			Nonrated operations	14N	Intelligence		1					1
			Other	IO/62E	Information operations or developmental engineering		1					1
	1YY/33Y/ 62E	Any operations, communications/ information, or developmental engineering	Nonrated operations	14N	Intelligence				1			1
	1YY/62EYF	Any operations or flight test developmental engineering	None	None	None				1			1
	1YY/63A	Any operations or acquisition management	None	None	None	1						1
	1YY/65F/ 65W	Any operations, financial management, or cost analysis	Nonrated operations	16R	Plans/programs	1						1
	1YY/65Y	Any operations or finance	Nonrated operations	16R	Plans/programs					1		1
	21B/63A	Equipment maintenance or acquisition management	None	None	None				3			3
	2YY/63A	Any logistics or acquisition management	None	None	None		1		1			2

Table A.1—Continued

Required Primary Skill Category	Required Primary Skill Code	Required Primary Skill	Required Secondary Skill Category	Required Secondary Skill Code	Required Secondary Skill	Required Experience Level(s): Any	1st Job	1st or 2nd	2nd Job	2nd or Senior	Senior Job	Total
	2YY/63A/64P	Any logistics, acquisition management, or contracting	None	None	None	1						1
	32E/33Y/62E/63A	Civil engineering, communications/information, developmental engineering, or acquisition management	None	None	None	1						1
	33Y/63A	Communications/information or acquisition management	Nonrated operations	16P	International political-military affairs				1			1
	33Y/6YY	Communications/information or acquisition/financial management	Acquisition and finance	6YY	Acquisition/financial management	1						1
	Acq/2YY	Any acquisition or any logistics	Other	86M/86P	Operations management or C2				1			1
	Any	Any	None	None	None	90	52	65	104	63	80	454
			Family of operations	APE	Aerospace power employment	2						2
				IO	Information operations	11	1		2	1		15
				MO	Mobility operations				1			1
			Nonrated operations	13S	Space or missile				2			2
				13SYD/E	Space surveillance or space warning						2	2
				14N	Intelligence	1		5	3	3	1	13
				16F/16P	Foreign area or international political-military affairs	2			1			3
				16P	International political-military affairs	5	5		9		2	21
				16R	Plans/programs	7			3		3	13

Table A.1—Continued

						Required Experience Level(s)						
Required Primary Skill Category	Required Primary Skill Code	Required Primary Skill	Required Secondary Skill Category	Required Secondary Skill Code	Required Secondary Skill	Any	1st Job	1st or 2nd	2nd Job	2nd or Senior	Senior Job	Total
			Support and OSI	32E	Civil engineering				1			1
				33Y	Communications and information systems		1		2			3
				36P	Personnel	1		2	3		4	10
				36P/38M	Personnel or manpower	1			1			2
			Other	Acq/2YY	Any acquisition or any logistics	1			1		2	4
	FBA/63A	Fighter, bomber, airlift, or acquisition management	None	None	None	1			1			2
	RT/13M	Any rated or airfield operations	None	None	None	1	1		1			3
	RT/13S	Any rated, space, or missile	None	None	None	1						1
			Other	Acq/2YY	Any acquisition or any logistics				1			1
	RT/13Y	Any rated, space, missile, or C2	None	None	None	3	9		10		3	25
			Nonrated operations	16R	Plans/programs	2	3					5
	RT/13Y/14N	Any rated, space, missile, C2, or intelligence	None	None	None				2			2
	RT/14N	Any rated or intelligence	Nonrated operations	16R	Plans/programs	1						1
	RT/21G	Any rated or logistics plans	None	None	None		1					1
	RT/21M	Any rated or munitions and missile maintenance	Acquisition and finance	6YY	Acquisition/financial management	1	1		1	1		4
	RT/2YY	Any rated or any logistics	Acquisition and finance	63A	Acquisition management	1	3	1	8		26	39
Other total						211	108	79	217	76	133	824
Unknown	Unknown	Unknown	Unknown	Unknown	Unknown	5						5
Unknown total						5						5
Grand total						737	491	186	843	133	388	2,778

APPENDIX B

Linear Optimization Model

This steady-state formulation reflects occupations, tracks, tiers and selectivity, but not uncertainty or learning.

Sets

Sets represent characteristics of either personnel inventory or the jobs they fill; they appear only in lower case.

p = inventory primary skill ∈ {*11F, 11B, 12F, 12B, 13SYA, 13YC, 14N, 62E, 63A, …*}
s = inventory paired or secondary skill ∈ {*13SYA, 13SYC, 14N, 21R, 36P, 63A, APE, MO, IO, …*}
t = inventory track ∈ {*fast, not-fast*}
k = inventory experience tier ∈ {*1st, 2nd, sr*}
rp = job primary skill requirement ∈ {*any, rated, FB, 11F, 2YY, 36P, 6YY, any acq, …*}
rs = job paired skill requirement ∈ {*none, 1YY, 13S, 14N, 2YY, 21M, 36P, 6YY, …*}
rt = job track requirement ∈ {*fast, not-fast*}
rk = preferred experience tier(s) ∈ {*1st, 1st or 2nd, 2nd, 2nd or sr, sr, any*}

Parameters

These are the constants relating to the "physics" of and objectives for the personnel flow and inventory; they appear in mixed upper and lower case.

Ret(t,k) = retention rate = fraction of those on track *t* entering tier *1st* who also enter tier *k*
Stay(t,k) = average tenure in tier *k* of a colonel on track *t*
Njobs(rp,rs,rt,rk) = number of jobs requiring occupations *(rp,rs)* and track *rt* during tier *rk*
Share(p) = proportion of O-6 officers in FY 2005 that were in primary occupation *p*
NoSecFrac(p) = fraction of the entering cohort in primary occupation *p* who have no secondary
Track_Purity = fraction of each category of fast-track jobs that must be filled by fast-track inventory. Its default value is 100%.

Tier_Purity = fraction of each category of jobs at each tier that must be filled by inventory from the designated tier(s) (e.g., *1st* filled by *1st*, *1st* or *2nd* filled by *1st*). Its default value is 100%.
Min_GO_Inflow(p,s) = required minimum flow of senior O-6 personnel into O-7 with the given *(p,s)* pair
GO_Purity = fraction of the inflow to brigadier general that must be filled by fast-track personnel. Its default value is 100%.
GO_Mult = multiplier for the brigadier general inflow constraint; serves as a sensitivity mechanism for augmenting the size of the pool from which this inflow is drawn. Its default value is unity.

Subsets and Validation Sets

Because the O-6 jobs (at least in 2002) were fairly flexible in their *(rp,rs)* pairings, we start by allowing only perfect matches of inventory *(p,s)* to job requirements *(rp,rs)*. This does not mean that *p* and *rp* need be identical. Rather, *p* must be consistent with *rp*, as *p* = *11F* = *fighter pilot* is consistent with *rp* = *rated.*

prpok(p,rp) = {*p consistent with rp*}
srsok(s,rs) = {*s consistent with rs*}
matchok(p,s,rp,rs) = {*(p,s)* consistent with *(rp,rs)*}; a match is deemed consistent if:

- *prpok* = *yes* for the *(p,rp)* pair
- *srsok* = *yes* for the *(s,rs)* pair
- a job exists in *Njobs* with the primary/secondary pair *(rp,rs)*
- a job exists in *Njobs* with the primary/secondary pair *(p,s)*.

The fourth condition allows *(p,s)* pairs in the inventory only if they are required for one or more jobs. The flexibility exists here, however, to add extra pairs to this pool if we wish.

ontier(k,rk) = {inventory tiers *k* that are always allowed to fill jobs that require tier(s) *rk*}
invalid_match(t,k,rt,rk) = {inventory track and tier *(t,k)* pairs that may never fill requirements possessing the requirement pair *(rt,rk)*}
assignok(p,s,t,k,rp,rs,rt,rk) = {set of valid inventory tuples *(p,s,t,k)* that may be assigned to the job requirement tuple *(rp,rs,rt,rk)*}. Assignments are allowed when

- *matchok(p,s,rp,rs)* = *yes*
- *invalid_match(t,k,rt,rk)* = *no*

invok(p,s,t,k) = {inventory tuples *(p,s,t,k)* which are valid}; the inventory element *(p,s,t,k)* is valid when *assignok* = *yes* for at least one *(rp,rs,rt,rk)*
multik(rk,rk´) = {job tiers *rk´* counted in selectivity for jobs in tier *rk*}.

When *rk* is a unique job tier (i.e., *1st, 2nd,* or *sr*), one should only consider the identical *rk´* for filling selectivity requirements for that job. The valid *multik* elements here would thus be {*1st,1st*}, {*2nd,2nd*}, and {*sr,sr*}. However, when *rk* is nonspecific (i.e., *1st or 2nd, 2nd or sr,* or *any*), more than one *rk´* needs to enter the selectivity computation. For example, the valid *rk´* elements for *multik* (*1st or 2nd, rk´*) are *rk´* = {*1st, 2nd, 1st, or 2nd*}. We allow limited compromises in matches with positions' requirements for both experience tiers and fast-track officers (see the constraints, below).

Variables

Variables fall into three categories. First, decision variables are the key players in the optimization itself. Second, dependent variables are factors of interest that can be readily derived from the values of the decision variables. Finally, the objective variables form the vector of possible optimal outcomes of the model. All three categories appear in upper case.

Decision Variables

ENTRANTS(p,s,t) = average annual number of O-6 entrants with primary skill *p* and paired skill *s* who follow track *t*

ASSIGN(p,s,t,k,rp,rs,rt,rk) = number of colonels of type *(p,s,t)* assigned during tier *k* to jobs requiring *(rp,rs,rt,rk)*.

Dependent Variables

FLOW(p,s,t,k) = *ENTRANTS(p,s,t)* * *Ret(t,k)* = annual inflow to tier *k* with *(p,s)* on track *t*

INV(p,s,t,k) = *FLOW(p,s,t,k)* * *Stay(t,k)* = inventory with occupations *(p,s)* on track *t* in tier *k*.

Objective Variables

Technically, only scalars may be objectives. Here, however, we also present some vectors that factor directly into the scalar quantities of interest.

MAXSEL = the minimum selectivity *–1* obtained (or sought) across all jobs

Rather than using *MAXSEL* as a true variable, we set it to a constant value of 2.0 (which corresponds to three faces assignable to any one open job) and observe the shortfalls, if any, from this target, as indicated in the next few variables.

POSSELSLACK(rp,rs,rt,rk) = amount by which selectivity exceeds *MAXSEL+1* in a given job

NEGSELSLACK(rp,rs,rt,rk) = amount selectivity falls short of *MAXSEL+1* target in a given job

TOTUNDERSEL1 = the sum of the negative selectivity slacks (a variant of the L_1 norm)

TOTUNDERSEL2 = the most negative selectivity slack (the L_∞ norm)

PRIMDEVHI(p) = upward deviation of the entering cohort's primary share from its target

PRIMDEVLO(p) = downward deviation of the entering cohort's primary share from its target

TOTPRIMDEV = sum of the upward and downward deviations from the primary target shares (the L_1 norm)

SECDEVHI(p) = upward deviation of the "no secondary" fraction in each primary group in the entering cohort from the global average
SECDEVLO(p) = downward deviation of the "no secondary" fraction in each primary group in the entering cohort from the global average
TOTSECDEV = sum of the upward and downward deviations from the global "no secondary" target (another L_1 norm).

These secondary targets are described in more detail in the section on their governing equations.

TOTINV = the total O-6 inventory.

As with *MAXSEL*, this could become a true variable. However, in the current formulation, *TOTINV* is fixed to equal the sum of *Njobs*.

NOSECENTRANTS = the number of *ENTRANTS* with $s = \{none\}$
FLEXCATS = a measure of the assignment flexibility of the incoming O-6 cohort
FASTTRACKS = the total number of fast-track entrants to the O-6 force.

Constraints

The relationships described below represent the problem's physics and policy relationships.

Fill All Jobs

$$\sum_{\substack{p,s,t,k \in \\ assignok(p,s,t,k,rp,rs,rt,rk)}} ASSIGN\left(p,s,t,k,rp,rs,rt,rk\right) = Njobs(rp,rs,rt,rk)$$

In a more constrained problem, we could change the equality to ≥. However, in the current formulation, the problem is feasible with strict equality, and jobs are not overfilled.

Inventory Must Cover the Assignments

For each *p,s,t,k* satisfying *invok(p,s,t,k)*,

$$\sum_{\substack{rp,rs,rt,rk \in \\ assignok(p,s,t,k,rp,rs,rt,rk)}} ASSIGN\left(p,s,t,k,rp,rs,rt,rk\right) = ENTRANTS\left(p,s,t\right) \times Ret\left(t,k\right) \times Stay\left(t,k\right)$$

Limit Off-Track Assignments

For each *Njobs(rp,rs,rt,rk)* > *0*, and $t = rt = fast$,

$$\sum_{\substack{(p,s,k)\in \\ assignok(p,s,t,k,rp,rs,rt,rk)}} ASSIGN(p,s,t,k,rp,rs,rt,rk) \geq$$

$$Track\_Purity \times \sum_{\substack{(p,s,t',k)\in \\ assignok(p,s,t',k,rp,rs,rt,rk)}} ASSIGN(p,s,t',k,rp,rs,rt,rk)$$

So far, we have chosen to limit only *not-fast-track* personnel filling *fast-track* jobs. It would be equally feasible to limit the number of *fast-trackers* filling *not-fast-track* jobs.

Limit Off-Tier Assignments

For each *Njobs(rp,rs,rt,rk)* > 0,

$$\sum_{\substack{(p,s,t,k)\in \\ assignok(p,s,t,k,rp,rs,rt,rk)\, and\, ontier(k,rk)}} ASSIGN(p,s,t,k,rp,rs,rt,rk) \geq$$

$$Tier\_Purity \times \sum_{\substack{(p,s,t,k)\in \\ assignok(p,s,t,k,rp,rs,rt,rk)}} ASSIGN(p,s,t,k,rp,rs,rt,rk)$$

In this formulation, we limit the number of colonels who can serve in adjacent experience tiers. We could broaden the scope to include *1st*-tier personnel serving in *sr* jobs or *sr* colonels serving in *1st*-tier jobs. If desired, these larger tier jumps could have a different limit, thereby expanding the limit constant to a vector, *Tier_Purity(k,rk)*.

Maintain an Appropriate O-7 Inflow

For each *(p,s)* pair where a brigadier general inflow must be satisfied (i.e., *Min_GO_Inflow* > *0*),

$$\sum_{t} ENTRANTS(p,s,t) \times Ret(t,\text{'}sr\text{'}) \geq Min\_GO\_Inflow(p,s) \times GO\_Mult$$

Maintain Purity of Track in Candidates Flowing into the O-7 Force

Candidates satisfying the brigadier general requirements must also satisfy the desired track balance.

$$ENTRANTS(p,s,\text{'}fast\text{'}) \times Ret(\text{'}fast\text{'},\text{'}sr\text{'}) \geq$$
$$Min\_GO\_Inflow(p,s) \times GO\_Mult \times GO\_Purity$$

Define Job Selectivity

Although we have explored alternative descriptions, we aim to maintain selectivity of at least *MAXSEL+1* as follows:

For each *rp,rs,rt,rk* where a job exists *(Njobs > 0)*,

$$\sum_{\substack{p,s,t,k\in \\ assignok(p,s,t,k,rp,rs,rt,rk)}} ENTRANTS(p,s,t)\times Ret(t,k) =$$

$$\sum_{\substack{p,s,t,k,rk'\in \\ assignok(p,s,t,k,rp,rs,rt,rk') \\ and\ multik(rk,rk')}} \frac{ASSIGN(p,s,t,k,rp,rs,rt,rk')}{Stay(t,k)} + MAXSEL$$

$$+POSSELSLACK(rp,rs,rt,rk) + NEGSELSLACK(rp,rs,rt,rk)$$

That is, the inflowing O-6 population (i.e., those individuals who are available for a new job assignment in the required tier *rk*, measured in people per year) must equal or exceed the average annual job openings plus a selectivity add-on. Deviations from that target are measured using slack variables. As their names suggest, *POSSELSLACK* must be positive (or zero), whereas *NEGSELSLACK* must be negative (or zero). *POSSELSLACK* is simply an accounting variable; it comes into play when we wish to see how much selectivity a given job has beyond the target. *NEGSELSLACK* determines how far below the desired selectivity target the job of interest has gone, if any.

Enforce Track Purity in Selectivity Computations

In a fashion very similar to its regulation in the inventory, track purity must also enter the computation of selectivity.

For each *rp,rs,rk* where a fast-track job exists *(Njobs > 0)*,

$$\sum_{\substack{p,s,k\in \\ assignok(p,s,'fast',k,rp,rs,'fast',rk)}} ENTRANTS(p,s,'fast')\times Ret('fast',k) \geq$$

$$\sum_{\substack{p,s,t,k,rk'\in \\ assignok(p,s,t,k,rp,rs,'fast',rk') \\ and\ multik(rk,rk')}} \frac{ASSIGN(p,s,t,k,rp,rs,'fast',rk')}{Stay(t,k)} \times Track\_Purity + MAXSEL$$

$$+NEGSELSLACK(rp,rs,'fast',rk)$$

Enforce Tier Purity in Selectivity Computations

Tier purity must also come into play when computing selectivity. For each *rp,rs,rt,rk* where a job exists *(Njobs > 0)*,

$$\sum_{\substack{p,s,t,k \in \\ assignok(p,s,t,k,rp,rs,rt,rk) \\ and\ ontier(k,rk)}} ENTRANTS(p,s,t) \times Ret(t,k) \geq$$

$$\sum_{\substack{p,s,t,k,rk' \subset \\ assignok(p,s,t,k,rp,rs,rt,rk') \\ and\ multik(rk,rk')}} \frac{ASSIGN(p,s,t,k,rp,rs,rt,rk')}{Stay(t,k)} \times Tier\_Purity + MAXSEL$$

$$+ NEGSELSLACK(rp,rs,rt,rk)$$

Objectives

As with many complex personnel systems, this problem has multiple goals. Rather than lumping objectives into a single, complex relationship, we are using sequential optimization. As could be expected, the order in which the objectives are invoked plays a key role in shaping the optimal space.

Maximize the Number of Entrants with No Paired (Secondary) Skill

$$Max\ NOSECENTRANTS = \sum_{\substack{p,t \in \\ invok(p,'none',t,'1st')}} ENTRANTS(p,'none',t)$$

We include this objective as a proxy for the difficulties the personnel community might encounter in fostering the development of paired skills in the personnel inventory below O-6. Such development may take some officers out of their career fields, probably diminishing productivity for a while, and, people may perceive, reducing their opportunities to develop further and excel within their occupational mainstreams.

Maximize the Flexibility of the Entering O-6 Cohort

$$Max\ FLEXCATS = \sum_{\substack{p,s,t \in \\ invok(p,s,t,'1st')}} \left(ENTRANTS(p,s,t) \times \sum_{\substack{pp,ss \in \\ matchok(pp,ss,p,s)}} 1 \right)$$

This flexibility score sums the products of the numbers of entrants and the numbers of *inventory* pairs that are consistent with them. Other measures of flexibility could be used as easily.

Minimize the Number of Entrants on the Fast Track

$$Min\ FASTTRACKS = \sum_{\substack{p,s\in \\ invok(p,s,'fast','1st')}} ENTRANTS(p,s,'fast')$$

Minimize the Total O-6 Inventory

$$Min\ TOTINV = \sum_{\substack{p,s,t\in \\ invok(p,s,t,'1st')}} ENTRANTS(p,s,t)\times Ret(t,k)\times Stay(t,k)$$

We currently fix *TOTINV* to equal the sum of *Njobs*. As noted above, should the formulation become more constrained, we can reinstate this as a true objective.

Minimize the Worst Shortfall in Selectivity

For each *rp,rs,rt,rk* satisfying *Njobs*>0,

$$TOTUNDERSEL2 \geq NEGSELSLACK(rp,rs,rt,rk)$$
$$Min\ TOTUNDERSEL2$$

Currently, we determine the worst selectivity shortfall and then bound each subsequent optimization with this value. Typically, the next objective is to minimize the overall selectivity shortfall, whose sum is subsequently bounded, as shown next.

Minimize the Overall Shortfall in Selectivity

$$Min\ TOTUNDERSEL1 = \sum_{rp,rs,rt,rk} NEGSELSLACK(rp,rs,rt,rk)$$

The variables *NEGELSLACK(rp,rs,rt,rk)* are not weighted by the numbers of jobs *Njobs(rp,rs,rt,rk) in this sum because the lowest selectivity for each (rp,rs,rt,rk) group is for the last job filled in the group, not for the others.*

Compute the Deviations from Primary Category Share Targets, Then Minimize Their Sum

$$PRIMDEVHI(p) \geq Share(p)\times \sum_{p',s,t,k\in invok(p',s,t,k)} INV(p',s,t,k) - \sum_{p',s,t,k\in invok(p',s,t,k)\ and\ prpok(p',p)} INV(p',s,t,k)$$

$$PRIMDEVLO(p) \geq -Share(p) \times \sum_{p',s,t,k \in invok(p',s,t,k)} INV(p',s,t,k) + \sum_{p',s,t,k \in invok(p',s,t,k)\ and\ prpok(p',p)} INV(p',s,t,k)$$

$$Min\ TOTPRIMDEV = \sum_{p \forall Share(p)>0} \left(PRIMDEVHI(p) + PRIMDEVLO(p)\right)$$

Find the Deviations from the Entering Cohort's "No Secondary" Average, Then Minimize Their Sum

This objective is a little tricky to keep linear. It depends explicitly on an existing solution, so this objective must not come first in the objective sequence. The idea is to compute the entry cohort's fraction of individuals with no secondary *(NoSecFrac)*—that is, no paired skill. The cohort is then broken down into its constituent primary categories, where the fraction of "no secondary" in each of these subgroups is to come as close to the global average as possible. The idea is to prevent any one primary category from attracting the bulk of individuals without paired skills.

$$SECDEVHI(p) \geq NoSecFrac \times \sum_{s,t \in invok(p,s,t,'1st')} ENTRANTS(p,s,t) - \sum_{p,s,t \in invok(p,'none',t,'1st')} ENTRANTS(p,'none',t)$$

$$SECDEVLO(p) \geq -NoSecFrac \times \sum_{s,t \in invok(p,s,t,'1st')} ENTRANTS(p,s,t) + \sum_{p,s,t \in invok(p,'none',t,'1st')} ENTRANTS(p,'none',t)$$

$$Min\ TOTSECDEV = \sum_{p} \left(SECDEVHI(p) + SECDEVLO(p)\right)$$

Sequencing of Objectives

The order of the individual objectives plays an important role in shaping the overall solution. At worst, objectives may be in direct conflict, such as minimizing the inventory and maximizing the entering cohort's flexibility rating (more entrants raises the score). At best, bounding the problem with an objective early in the sequence can significantly limit the feasible possibilities that remain for subsequent metrics of interest. The model has typically been run with objectives in the following order:

0. Minimize the total inventory (if the inventory is not explicitly equated to the sum of jobs).
1. Minimize the worst selectivity shortfall.
2. Minimize the sum of selectivity shortfalls in all categories.
3. Maximize the number of entrants without a paired skill.
4. Minimize the total deviation from primary category targets.
5. Minimize the number of fast-track entrants.
6. Maximize the entering cohort's total flexibility score.
7. Minimize the total deviation from the "no secondary" target.

APPENDIX C

Matches with Occupational Requirements

Many or few combinations (and sometimes only one combination) of primary and paired (or secondary) skills (*p,s*) on the inventory or supply side may match a combination of primary and paired skills (*rp,rs*) demanded on the requirements side. The specific combinations allowed in the flow analysis—that is, which kinds of inventory were allowed to fill the various kinds of jobs—were delineated using these four logical rules:

- Allow (*p,s*) to fill (*rp,rs*) if *p* matches *rp* and *s* matches *rs*.
- The (*p,s*) combinations in the previous rule should include all of the required (*rp,rs*) combinations, but no others.
- Allow (*p,None*) to fill (*rp,rs*) if *rp* = *Any* and *p* = *rs*.
- Allow (*14N,s*) to fill (*14N/33S,14N*), regardless of *s*.

Table C.1 shows several examples where the required primary skill was FB (fighter or bomber). The more categories of positions whose primary and paired skills matched the required combination of primary and paired skill, the more categories of colonels (or inventory) that were eligible to meet the requirement. For example, 11 combinations matched the requirement for FB primary skill and Acq/2YY (any acquisition or any logistics) paired skill, but only two matched the requirement for FB primary skill and the IO (information operations) paired skill. Although additional combinations of primary and paired skills could meet these requirements in practice (e.g., 11B with paired skill 63A), the model need not consider them explicitly because it reflects them implicitly (11B with paired skill 63A is implicit in 11B/12B with paired skill 63A) and because it found practical ways to meet all requirements without them. Inventory in only the combinations that were explicitly required proved sufficient.[1]

[1] We experimented with allowing the model substantial numbers of specific skill pairings that were not demanded explicitly—for example, combinations such as 11B with paired skill 63A—but they scarcely affected the optimal solutions.

Table C.1
Matches for Some Positions Requiring Fighter or Bomber (FB) Primary Skill

Colonel's (inventory's) Matching Occupational Skills				Position Required This Paired Skill			
Primary Skill		Paired (or Secondary) Skill		APE	IO	Acq	Acq/2YY
11B/12B	Bomber	APE	Aerospace power employment	x			
		IO	Information operations		x		
		21R	Logistics readiness				x
		63A	Acquisition management			x	x
		Acq/2YY	Any acquisition or any logistics				x
		RQ	Requirements			x	x
		T&E	Test and evaluation			x	x
11F	Fighter pilot	APE	Aerospace power employment	x			
		Acq	Any acquisition			x	x
1YF	Fighter	APE	Aerospace power employment	x			
		63A	Acquisition management			x	x
		Acq	Any acquisition			x	x
		T&E	Test and evaluation			x	x
FB	Fighter or bomber	APE	Aerospace power employment	x			
		IO	Information operations		x		
		Acq	Any acquisition			x	x
		Acq/2YY	Any acquisition or any logistics				x
			No. of matches	4	2	8	11

APPENDIX D

Detailed Occupational Inflow Floors

Table D.1
Minimum Average Number of New Colonels per Year

Primary Skill		Paired Skill		Solution	
				Marginal	Preferred
11A	Airlift pilot	None	None	15.3	11.1
11A total				15.3	11.1
11B	Bomber pilot	6YY	Acquisition/financial management	1.2	2.4
11B total				1.2	2.4
11B/12B	Bomber	13SYA/B/D/E	Any space	.0	.0
		16P	International political-military affairs	.7	1.4
		16R	Plans/programs	.3	.5
		21R	Logistics readiness	.3	.6
		63A	Acquisition management	.5	1.0
		APE	Aerospace power employment	1.1	2.2
		IO	Information operations	.5	.2
		None	None	1.1	
		RQ	Requirements	.1	.3
		T&E	Test and evaluation	.1	.3
11B/12B total				4.7	6.5
11B/12B/13SYC	Bomber or missile	14N	Intelligence	.2	.5
11B/12B/13SYC total				.2	.5
11E	Experimental-test pilot	62EYF	Flight test developmental engineering	1.2	2.3
11E total				1.2	2.3
11F	Fighter pilot	16R	Plans/programs	1.5	3.0
		Acq	Any acquisition	2.1	2.6
		APE	Aerospace power employment	1.3	2.6
		None	None	17.6	14.8
11F total				22.6	22.9
11F/11B	Fighter or bomber pilot	None	None	5.2	
11F/11B total				5.2	

Table D.1—Continued

Primary Skill		Paired Skill		Solution	
				Marginal	Preferred
11F/11H	Fighter or helicopter pilot	None	None	8.0	5.9
11F/11H total				8.0	5.9
11H	Helicopter pilot	None	None	1.3	2.6
11H total				1.3	2.6
11H/11S/12S	Helicopter pilot or SOF	16R	Plans/programs	.5	.2
		None	None	1.6	
11H/11S/12S total				2.1	.2
11R	Reconnaissance pilot	None	None	1.4	2.7
11R total				1.4	2.7
11S/12S	Special operations	16P	International political-military affairs	.1	.2
		16R	Plans/programs	1.2	2.3
		21R	Logistics readiness	.4	.8
		36P/38M	Personnel or manpower	.5	1.0
		6YY	Acquisition/financial management	1.3	2.7
		APE	Aerospace power employment	1.5	3.0
		None	None	.9	
11S/12S total				5.9	10.0
11Y	Pilot	2YY/63A	Any logistics or acquisition management	1.3	2.7
		36P/38M	Personnel or manpower	.8	1.6
		None	None	76.5	20.9
11Y total				78.6	25.2
13A	Astronaut	None	None	2.5	4.6
13A total				2.5	4.6
13B	Air battle manager	None	None	5.5	3.2
13B total				5.5	3.2
13D	Control and recovery	None	None	1.3	2.7
13D total				1.3	2.7
13M	Airfield operations	33Y	Communications and information systems	1.2	2.3
13M total				1.2	2.3
13S	Space or missile	16P	international political-military affairs	1.0	2.1
		16R	Plans/programs	.7	1.3
		APE	Aerospace power employment	.1	.2
		E&T	Education and training	1.2	2.4
		IO	Information operations	.4	.6
		None	None	2.1	
13S total				5.5	6.5
13SYA	Space satellite C2	Acq	Any acquisition	1.4	2.7
13SYA total				1.4	2.7

Table D.1—Continued

Primary Skill		Paired Skill		Solution Marginal	Solution Preferred
13SYA/B/D/E	Any space	13SYC	Missile	.2	.3
		14N	Intelligence	.0	.1
		16R	Plans/programs	.2	.3
		33Y	Communications and information systems	.3	.5
		63A	Acquisition management	.5	1.0
		APE	Aerospace power employment	1.2	2.4
		IO	Information operations	.2	.3
		RQ	Requirements	.2	.5
13SYA/B/D/E total				2.8	5.5
13SYA/D/E	Space satellite C2, surveillance, or warning	None	None	.1	
13SYA/D/E total				.1	
13SYB	Space lift	13SYC	Missile	1.4	2.7
		16R	Plans/programs	.5	1.0
		Acq	Any acquisition	1.5	2.9
13SYB total				3.3	6.5
13SYC	Missile	16P	International political-military affairs	.2	.3
		16R	Plans/programs	.2	.5
		21MYA	Munitions and missile maintenance, missile	2.0	3.6
		Acq	Any acquisition	1.2	2.3
		None	None	2.0	
13SYC total				5.6	6.6
13SYD	Space surveillance	Acq	Any acquisition	1.2	2.4
		None	None	.0	
13SYD total				1.3	2.4
14N	Intelligence	13S	Space or missile	1.2	2.4
		16F	Foreign area	1.3	2.7
		16P	International political-military affairs	.0	.0
		16R	Plans/programs	1.4	2.7
		33Y	Communications and information systems	.3	.8
		36P/38M	Personnel or manpower	.2	.5
		APE	Aerospace power employment	1.8	3.0
		E&T	Education and training	1.2	2.4
		IO	Information operations	2.4	4.2
		None	None	9.8	
14N total				19.7	18.8
14N/33Y	Intelligence or communications/information systems	14N	Intelligence	.2	
14N/33Y total				.2	

Table D.1—Continued

Primary Skill		Paired Skill		Solution	
				Marginal	Preferred
15W	Weather	16R	Plans/programs	1.4	2.7
		None	None	2.2	1.2
15W total				3.5	3.8
1YE	Experimental-test	63A	Acquisition management	.7	1.0
		APE	Aerospace power employment	.1	.3
		None	None	.1	
1YE total				1.0	1.3
1YF	Fighter	16P	International political-military affairs	2.0	3.9
		16R	Plans/programs	.3	.6
		63A	Acquisition management	.3	.6
		APE	Aerospace power employment	7.2	14.4
		E&T	Education and training	.3	.6
		T&E	Test and evaluation	.1	.3
1YF total				10.2	20.5
1YF/1YM	Fighter or mobility	None	None	.2	
1YF/1YM total				.2	
1YM	Mobility	16P	International political-military affairs	.3	.5
		16R	Plans/programs	2.0	4.3
		63A	Acquisition management	1.5	2.3
		Acq	Any acquisition		.8
		APE	Aerospace power employment	1.7	3.4
		MO	Mobility operations	1.4	2.7
1YM total				6.7	14.0
1YM/11S/12S	Mobility or SOF	None	None	.2	
1YM/11S/12S total				.2	
1YR	Reconnaissance	Acq	Any acquisition	.6	.9
1YR total				.6	.9
1YR/13B	Reconnaissance or ABM	13SYA/B/D/E	Any space	.1	.2
		16P	International political-military affairs	.1	.1
		APE	Aerospace power employment	.3	.6
		IO	Information operations	.3	.5
		RQ	Requirements	.0	.1
1YR/13B total				.7	1.4
1YR/14N	Reconnaissance or intelligence	63A	Acquisition management	1.3	2.7
1YR/14N total				1.3	2.7
1YT	Tanker	None	None	4.6	5.8
1YT total				4.6	5.8

Table D.1—Continued

Primary Skill		Paired Skill		Solution Marginal	Solution Preferred
21A	Aircraft maintenance	None	None	1.4	2.9
21A total				**1.4**	**2.9**
21A/B/M	Maintenance	21R	Logistics readiness	.5	1.1
		64P	Contracting	.5	1.0
21A/B/M total				**1.0**	**2.1**
21B	Equipment maintenance	13S	Space or missile	1.2	2.4
		21M	Munitions and missile maintenance	1.3	2.5
		32E	Civil engineering	1.2	2.4
		63A	Acquisition management	1.5	3.0
		E&T	Education and training	1.3	2.8
		None	None	14.7	15.1
21B total				**21.2**	**28.2**
21B/21R	Equipment maintenance or logistics readiness	63A	Acquisition management	2.3	
		None	None	4.0	.8
21B/21R total				**6.4**	**.8**
21G	Logistics plans	2YY	Any logistics	1.5	3.2
		Acq/21M	Any acquisition or equipment maintenance	1.2	2.3
21G total				**2.7**	**5.5**
21M	Munitions and missile maintenance	63A	Acquisition management	1.6	3.2
21M total				**1.6**	**3.2**
21MYA	Munitions and missile maintenance, missile	None	None	2.0	3.9
21MYA total				**2.0**	**3.9**
21MYB	Munitions and missile maintenance, spacelift	33Y	Communications and information systems	1.6	3.3
21MYB total				**1.6**	**3.3**
21R	Logistics readiness	16P	International political-military affairs	.2	.3
		16R	Plans/programs	.2	2.6
		21A/B/M	Maintenance	.8	1.7
		63A	Acquisition management	.2	.4
		65F	Financial management	.2	.4
		None	None	9.6	
21R total				**11.2**	**5.4**
21S	Supply	None	None	1.4	2.7
21S total				**1.4**	**2.7**
21T	Transportation	None	None	1.4	2.7
21T total				**1.4**	**2.7**
2YY	Any logistics	16R	Plans/programs	1.1	.1
2YY total				**1.1**	**.1**

Table D.1—Continued

Primary Skill		Paired Skill		Solution Marginal	Solution Preferred
31P	Security forces	21T/34M/ E&T	Transportation, services, or education/training	1.2	2.4
		None	None	5.8	9.1
31P total				7.0	11.5
32E	Civil engineering	16R	Plans/programs	.9	1.8
		None	None	12.7	16.5
32E total				13.6	18.3
33Y	Communications and information systems	13SYA/B/ D/E	Any space	.0	.0
		16P	International political-military affairs	1.3	2.7
		36P	Personnel	1.2	2.4
		IO	Information operations	3.1	2.3
		None	None	24.4	14.2
33Y total				30.0	21.6
34M	Services	None	None	4.3	7.4
34M total				4.3	7.4
35B	Band	None	None	.6	1.0
35B total				.6	1.0
35P	Public affairs	16P	International political-military affairs	1.8	3.5
		16R	Plans/programs	1.2	2.4
		None	None	.7	
35P total				3.7	5.9
36P	Personnel	13S	Space or missile	1.3	2.7
		33Y	Communications and information systems	1.3	2.7
		61S	Scientist	1.2	2.4
		None	None	15.7	
36P total				19.5	7.8
36P/38M	Personnel or manpower	16P	International political-military affairs	.2	.3
		16R	Plans/programs	1.2	2.3
		APE	Aerospace power employment	.4	.8
		E&T	Education and training	.6	1.2
36P/38M total				2.4	4.7
38M	Manpower	36P	Personnel	.6	1.2
		None	None	1.5	2.2
38M total				2.1	3.4
61S	Scientist	36P	Personnel	1.2	2.3
		63A	Acquisition management	1.5	3.8
		IO	Information operations	1.3	2.7
		None	None	2.4	
61S total				6.4	8.9

Table D.1—Continued

Primary Skill		Paired Skill		Solution Marginal	Solution Preferred
61S/62E	Scientist or developmental engineering	63A	Acquisition management	1.3	1.9
61S/62E total				1.3	1.9
61SYA	Analytical scientist	13S	Space or missile	1.2	2.3
61SYA total				1.2	2.3
62E	Developmental engineering	13S/14N	Space, missile, or intelligence	.6	.2
		13SYB/C	Space lift or missile	.5	.9
		Acq	Any acquisition	1.2	2.3
		None	None	7.6	3.3
62E total				9.9	6.6
63A	Acquisition management	13B	Air battle manager	.6	1.0
		13B/D/M	C2ISR	.8	1.7
		13SYA/B/D/E	Any space	.2	.4
		16P/16R	Plan/programs or international political-military affairs	1.5	3.2
		21A/B/M	Maintenance	.2	.4
		21R	Logistics readiness	.1	.3
		2YY	Any logistics	1.2	2.4
		33Y	Communications and information systems	.5	.8
		61S/62E	Scientist or developmental engineering	.8	1.3
		62E	Developmental engineering	1.3	2.6
		64P	Contracting	.0	.1
		65F	Financial management	.5	.8
		Acq	Any acquisition	.1	
		APE	Aerospace power employment	.1	.2
		IO	Information operations	.2	.4
		None	None	27.1	
63A total				35.3	15.6
64P	Contracting	13SYE	Space warning	1.2	2.3
		36P	Personnel	.7	1.3
		None	None	6.6	9.2
64P total				8.5	12.9
65F	Financial management	16R	Plans/programs	.4	.5
		16R/21R/33Y	Plans/programs, logistics readiness, or communications/information	.2	.7
		Acq	Any acquisition	1.2	2.3
		None	None	7.4	11.9
		SA	Safety	.1	.2
65F total				9.3	15.7

Table D.1—Continued

Primary Skill		Paired Skill		Solution	
				Marginal	Preferred
65W	Cost analysis	None	None	1.2	2.3
65W total				1.2	2.3
6YY	Acquisition/financial management	13SYC/21M	Missile or munitions and missile maintenance	1.2	2.4
		MO	Mobility operations	1.3	2.7
6YY total				2.5	5.1
71S	Special investigations	31P	Security forces	.5	.9
		None	None	3.7	7.1
71S total				4.1	8.0
Acq	Any acquisition	13SYA	Space satellite C2	2.4	4.3
		13SYB	Space lift	2.3	4.3
		13SYD	Space surveillance	1.2	2.3
Acq total				5.8	10.9
Acq/2YY	Any acquisition or any logistics	86M/86P	Operations management or C2	1.3	2.7
Acq/2YY total				1.3	2.7
FB	Fighter or bomber	IO	Information operations		.8
FB total					.8
FB/1YM	Fighter, bomber, or mobility	None	None	.3	
FB/1YM total				.3	
FB/1YM/11S/12S	Fighter, bomber, mobility, or SOF	None	None	.1	
FB/1YM/11S/12S total				.1	
RT	Any rated	14N	Intelligence	1.9	2.4
		16R	Plans/programs	1.3	
		EW	Electronic warfare	1.3	2.7
		IO	Information operations	.6	1.2
RT total				5.2	6.3
RT not 13B	Any rated except ABM	62E/63A	Developmental engineering or acquisition management	1.2	
RT not 13B total				1.2	
Unknown	Unknown	Unknown	Unknown	1.0	1.3
Unknown total				1.0	1.3
Grand total				457.9	448.5

APPENDIX E

Air Force Briefing Slides That Presented the Skill-Pairing Floors

This appendix displays elements from two briefings given in 2005: First (Slides 1–15), AF/DPP described for CFMs the effort to establish the floors and illustrated their application for the MAF; second (Slides 16–35), AFPC displayed graphically the percentage floors that emerged from this report's analysis, after AFPC's final adjustments listed in Chapter 5.

We have modified these slides in the following minor ways:

- added slide numbers to facilitate our references to the slides at the end of Chapter Five
- enlarged the type in Slides 10–12 and 16–35, making them easier to read
- added more gridlines and oriented the vertical axis labels horizontally instead of vertically in Slides 10 and 16–35, also making them easier to read
- added the labels "Preferred floor" and "Marginal floor" in Slides 10–12 and 16–35, clarifying and emphasizing that this work identified only two different floors for the shares of new colonels with each skill pair, not maximum and minimum percentages
- added the words "analytic methods" that seemed to be missing from the last bullet on Slide 15
- narrowed the bar widths (but did not change their lengths) in Slides 19, 22, 25–28, 30–31, and 33–35, making them look more like the others.

AF/DPP Briefing

Slide 1

Headquarters U.S. Air Force

Integrity - Service - Excellence

Force Development

Officer Skill Pairings

24 October 2005
Brig Gen Glenn Spears
AF/DPP

U.S. AIR FORCE

Slide 2

U.S. AIR FORCE

Officer Skill Pairings

- Purpose: Apprise officer career field managers of effort to establish officer occupational skill pairings and gain support to refine numbers

- Topics:
  - Force Development 101
  - History of Skill Pairings
  - Skill Pairing Example
  - Implementation Plan
  - Open Discussion

Right Person ... Right Place ... Right Time

Slide 3

U.S. AIR FORCE

Force Development 101

- Force Development emerged in 2002
- Key Tenets of Force Development:
  - Systematic process
  - Simultaneously developing occupational skills & enduring leadership competencies
  - Achieved through deliberate education, training, & experience
  - Has desired effects throughout leadership spectrum – tactical to strategic
  - Produces full-spectrum leaders filling expeditionary AF mission needs

The next two slides come from the Summer 2003 Force Development Spread the Word briefing

Right Person ... Right Place ... Right Time

Slide 4

U.S. AIR FORCE

What It Is and Is Not ...

- Force Development is about ...
  - Accomplishing AF missions *today* and *tomorrow*
  - Improving your skills deliberately
  - Using your skills more effectively
  - Listening to you better about your goals
  - Talking to you more clearly about your potential and possibilities
- Force Development is not about ...
  - Development for its own sake
  - Developing everyone the same
  - Just changing PME
  - Your career field alone
  - Your next promotion

Source: Officer Force Development World-wide Spread the Word Briefing, 2003

Right Person ... Right Place ... Right Time

U.S. AIR FORCE

Slide 5

Why Do We Need It In The AF ?

- Today
  - "Deep" perspective
  - Chance "development"
  - Focus on functional skills
  - Less focus on enduring competencies
  - Career stovepipes
- Tomorrow
  - "Wider" perspective
  - Systematic, deliberate development
  - Develop necessary functional skills and enduring competencies
  - Interchangeable senior leaders
  - Better team builders

Vector to requirements

Source: Officer Force Development World-wide Spread the Word Briefing, 2003

Right Person ... Right Place ... Right Time

U.S. AIR FORCE

Slide 6

Skill Pairing History

- Skill Pairings are an essential part of vectoring to requirements
  - Establishes the corporate skills goal for O6 entry pool demographics
  - Is the foundation for career fields to build upon to support the AFSC
- 2002: Goal of ensuring our senior leaders have right experience
  - Used GO jobs & O6 expert panels to identify senior officer primary and secondary skill requirements
  - Functionals, MAJCOMs, AFPC, and AFSLMO refined data
  - However, we stumbled in allocating flexible reqs, translating pairings into DT tools, & didn't fully screen for practicality = show stopper!!
- 2005+: Develop tools to implement more deliberate vectoring process
  - New O6 / GS-15 survey to determine requirement changes
  - Better refinement of flexible requirements and increased coordination with the stakeholders to ensure we are meeting the DT's needs

Right Person ... Right Place ... Right Time

Slide 7

U.S. AIR FORCE

FDC - Skill Pairing Working Group

Objectives

- **Examine the logical experience, education, and skill pairings across all line officers AFSCs**
- **Examine and recommend changes to improve the current skill pairing process**
- **Identify barriers to assignment of officers within the identified skill pairings**
- **Develop a comprehensive implementation plan to integrate the recommendations into the officer force development process**

Participants

- **Brig Gen Glenn Spears, AF/DPP (Chair)**
- **Col Jeffrey Fraser, AF/XOO (CAF/MAF)**
- **Col Wayne Hudson, AF/XOS (13S)**
- **Col John Stankowski, AF/ILM (21X)**
- **Mr Terry Scott, SAF/XCI, (33S)**
- **Ms Sherry Medders, SAF/PAR (35P)**
- **Mr Pat Hogan, SAF/AQX (62E/63A)**
- **Ms Glenda Scheiner, SAF/FMP (65X)**

Work with a sub-set of AFSCs to get sample feedback before going forward

Right Person ... Right Place ... Right Time

Slide 8

U.S. AIR FORCE

"Simplified" Skill Pairing Process

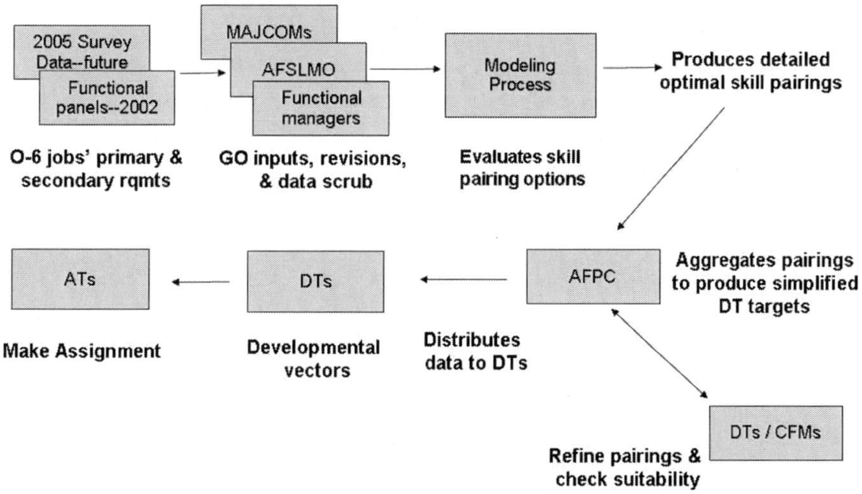

Right Person ... Right Place ... Right Time

U.S. AIR FORCE

Slide 9

MAF Example: 1990 Year Group

- 314 MAF officers in the 1990 year group (as of FY2004)
- Requirements model shows at least 22-50% of these officers need skill pairings
- For the 1990 year group that 22-50% breaks down as follows:

Skill Pair	Min # of Officers: Low	Min # of Officers: High
Plans/Programs	15	39
Aerospace Power Employment	14	33
Any Acquisition	16	32
Mobility Ops	11	25
Intelligence	4	6
Any Logistics/Acq Mgt	2	6
Information Ops	2	5
Personnel/Manpower	2	5
International Political-Military Affairs	2	5

Right Person ... Right Place ... Right Time

Slide 10

MAF Skill Pairing Targets

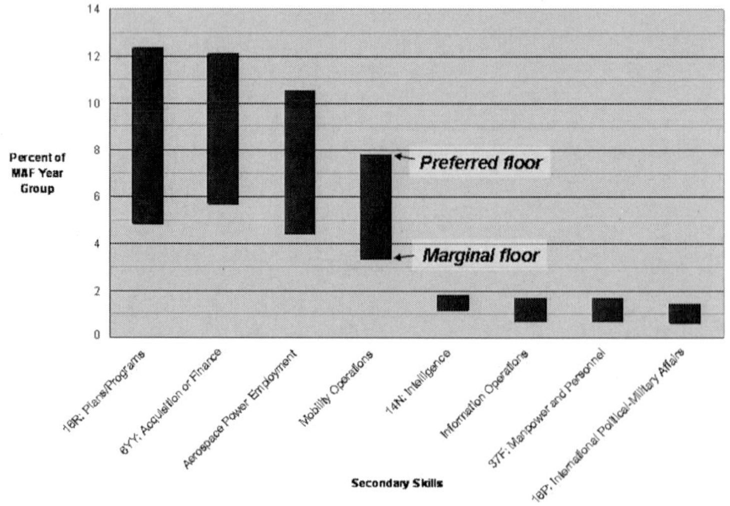

Integrity - Service - Excellence

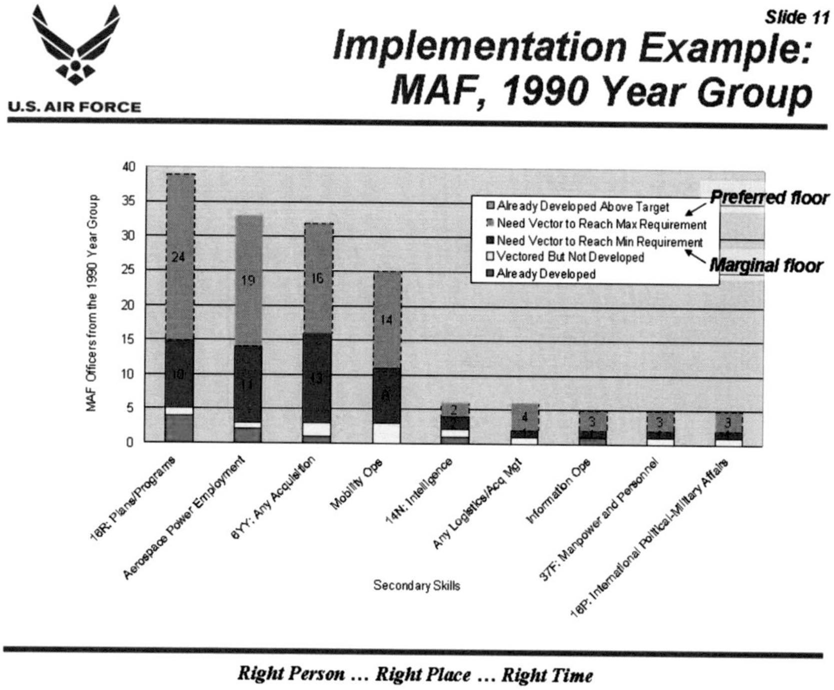
U.S. AIR FORCE
Slide 11
Implementation Example:
MAF, 1990 Year Group
Already Developed Above Target
Need Vector to Reach Max Requirement
Need Vector to Reach Min Requirement
Vectored But Not Developed
Already Developed
Preferred floor
Marginal floor
MAF Officers from the 1990 Year Group
40
35
30
25
20
15
10
5
0
24
19
16
14
10
11
13
8
2
4
3
3
3
16R: Plans/Programs
Aerospace Power Employment
6YY: Any Acquisition
Mobility Ops
14N: Intelligence
Any Logistics/Acq Mgt
Information Ops
37F: Manpower and Personnel
16P: International Political-Military Affairs
Secondary Skills
Right Person ... Right Place ... Right Time

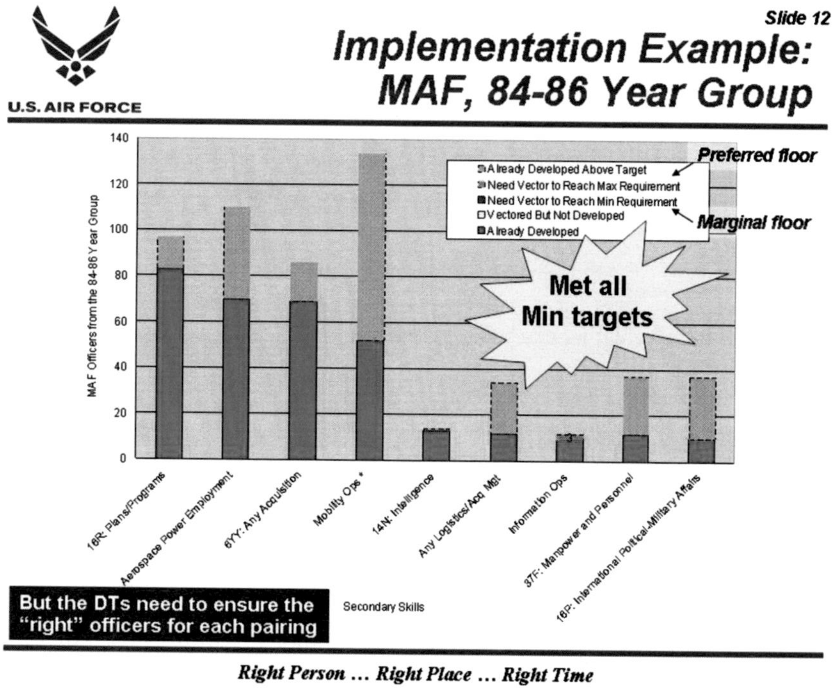
U.S. AIR FORCE
Slide 12
Implementation Example:
MAF, 84-86 Year Group
Already Developed Above Target
Need Vector to Reach Max Requirement
Need Vector to Reach Min Requirement
Vectored But Not Developed
Already Developed
Preferred floor
Marginal floor
Met all
Min targets
MAF Officers from the 84-86 Year Group
140
120
100
80
60
40
20
0
16R: Plans/Programs
Aerospace Power Employment
6YY: Any Acquisition
Mobility Ops *
14N: Intelligence
Any Logistics/Acq Mgt
Information Ops
37F: Manpower and Personnel
16P: International Political-Military Affairs
Secondary Skills
But the DTs need to ensure the "right" officers for each pairing
Right Person ... Right Place ... Right Time

U.S. AIR FORCE

Slide 13

Working Group Feedback

- Makes sense ... most of the secondary skills are closely related ... we've been doing a lot of this already
- But there is more to do as we begin to implement this process:
  - Establish common lexicon for skill pairing categories / "What is IO?"
  - Regularly address dynamic AFSCs and changes in job requirements
  - Formalize duty identifier award process to capture officer experience
  - Address complexities of small officer career fields
  - Formalize developmental assignment cross flow management
  - Continue to publicize the force development message, codify our processes, and institutionalize in our culture

Right Person ... Right Place ... Right Time

U.S. AIR FORCE

Slide 14

Implementation Way Ahead

- Oct 05: Present skill pairing overview to officer CFM & brief to all line DTs
- Continue to refine pairings with CFM / DT involvement and incorporate on-going survey data
  - As we work with the DT we ask your assistance in critically reviewing the occupational skill pairing targets for senior level suitability
- Obtain stakeholder feedback and make necessary process improvements
- Codify in policy

Right Person ... Right Place ... Right Time

Slide 15

U.S. AIR FORCE

Take Aways

- Skill pairings targets establish minimum corporate development goals which the career fields can use to build upon for vectoring
  - DTs may have valid secondary skills at O4 / O5 to meet
- Vector guide long-term shape of AF / career fields ... not just next job
- Not all officers need skill pairings and not all AFSCs will have skill pairings
  - Plenty of O6 jobs do not require skill pairings
  - Presence / lack of skill pairings has no relation to promotion potential
- Our skill pairings will continually evolve to meet dynamic field requirements & improved analytic methods

Right Person ... Right Place ... Right Time

AFPC Briefing Slides

Slide 16

CAF Skill Pairing Targets

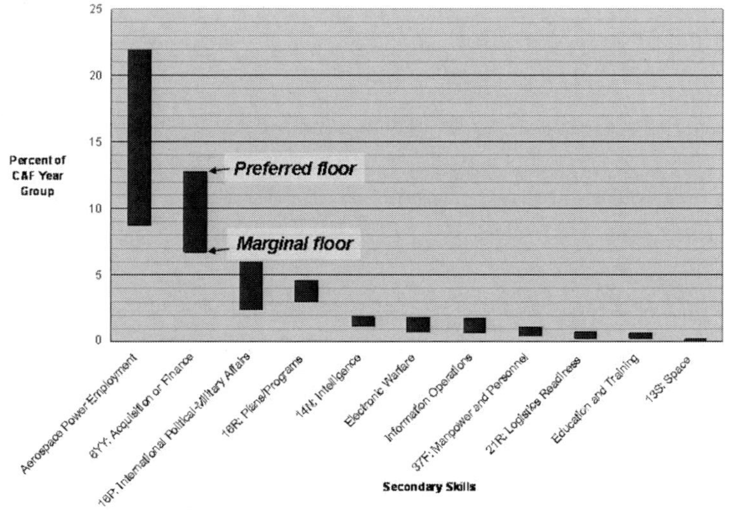

Integrity - Service - Excellence

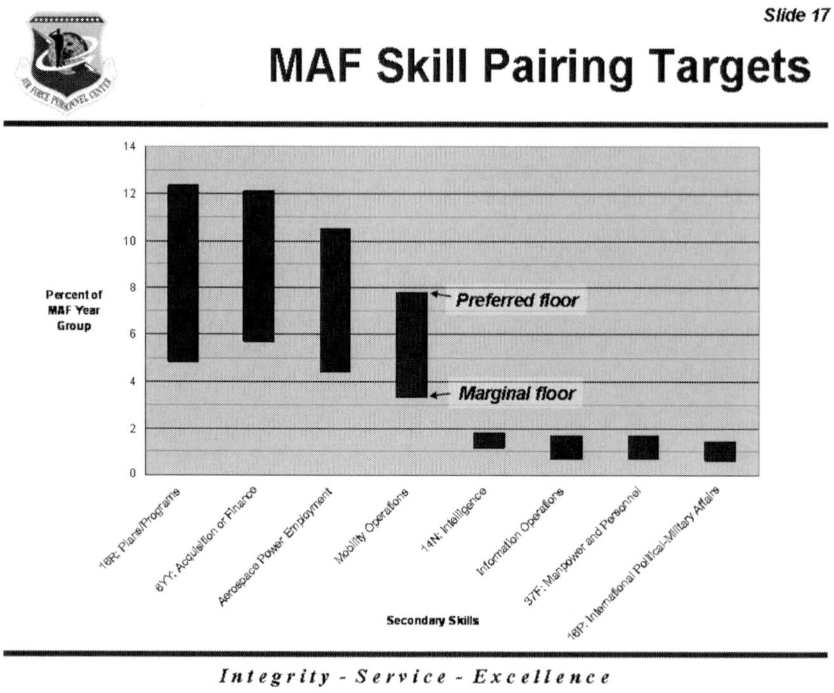
Slide 17
MAF Skill Pairing Targets
Percent of MAF Year Group
0
2
4
6
8
10
12
14
Preferred floor
Marginal floor
16R: Plans/Programs
6YY: Acquisition or Finance
Aerospace Power Employment
Mobility Operations
14N: Intelligence
Information Operations
37F: Manpower and Personnel
16P: International Political-Military Affairs
Secondary Skills
Integrity - Service - Excellence

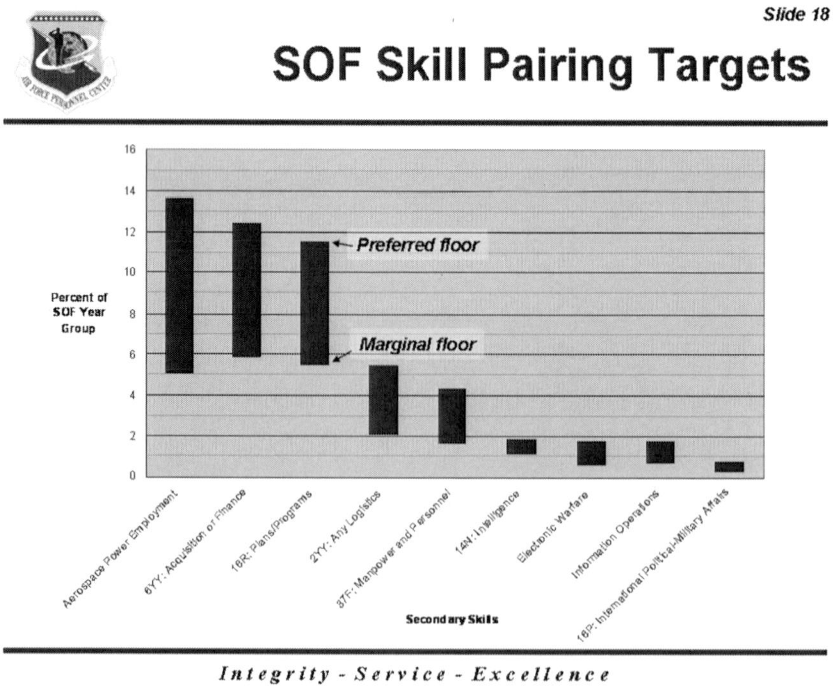
Slide 18
SOF Skill Pairing Targets
Percent of SOF Year Group
0
2
4
6
8
10
12
14
16
Preferred floor
Marginal floor
Aerospace Power Employment
6YY: Acquisition or Finance
16R: Plans/Programs
2YY: Any Logistics
37F: Manpower and Personnel
14N: Intelligence
Electronic Warfare
Information Operations
16P: International Political-Military Affairs
Secondary Skills
Integrity - Service - Excellence

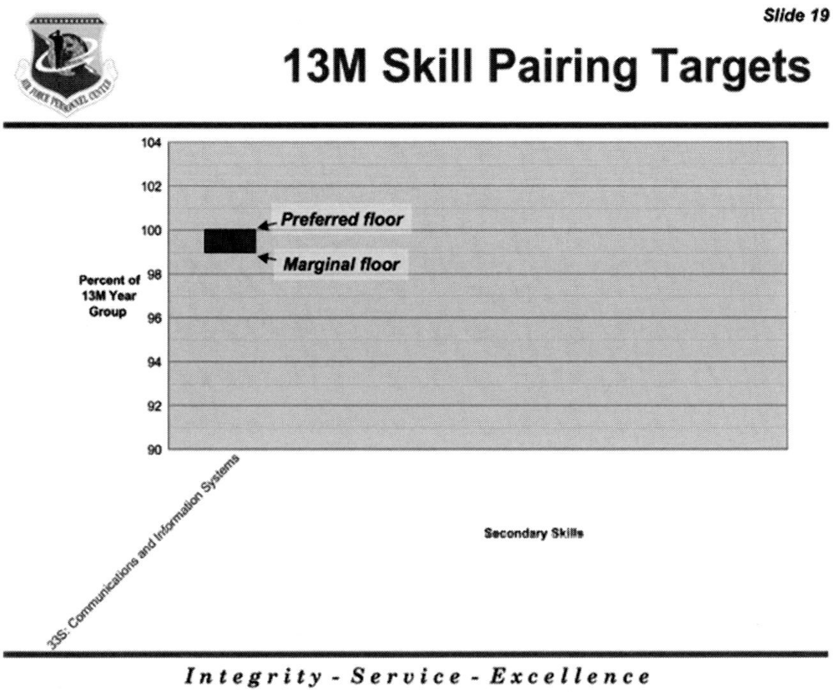
Slide 19
13M Skill Pairing Targets
104
102
100
98
96
94
92
90
Percent of 13M Year Group
Preferred floor
Marginal floor
33S: Communications and Information Systems
Secondary Skills
Integrity - Service - Excellence

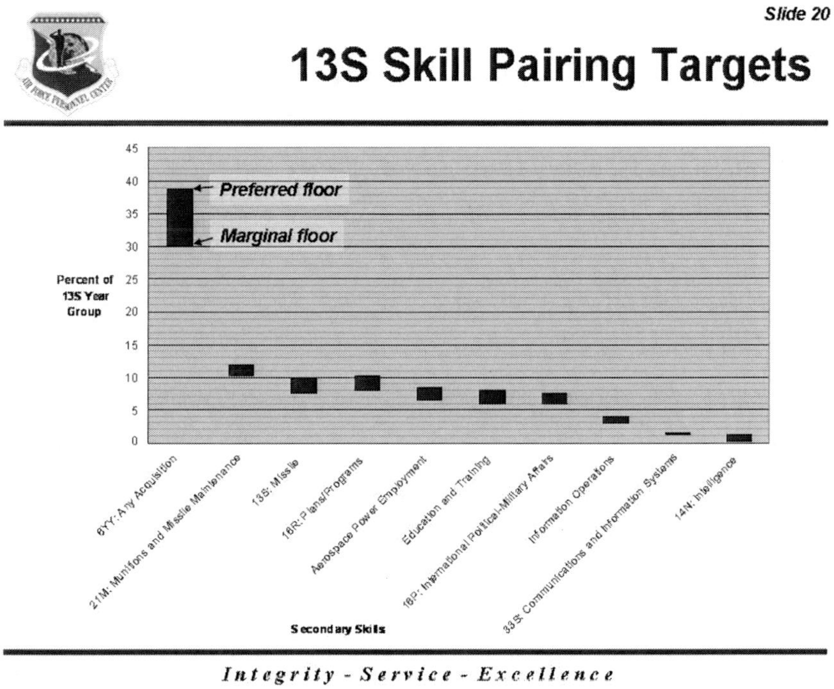
Slide 20
13S Skill Pairing Targets
45
40
35
30
25
20
15
10
5
0
Percent of 13S Year Group
Preferred floor
Marginal floor
6YY: Any Acquisition
21M: Munitions and Missile Maintenance
13S: Missile
16R: Plans/Programs
Aerospace Power Employment
Education and Training
16P: International Political-Military Affairs
Information Operations
33S: Communications and Information Systems
14N: Intelligence
Secondary Skills
Integrity - Service - Excellence

Slide 21

14N Skill Pairing Targets

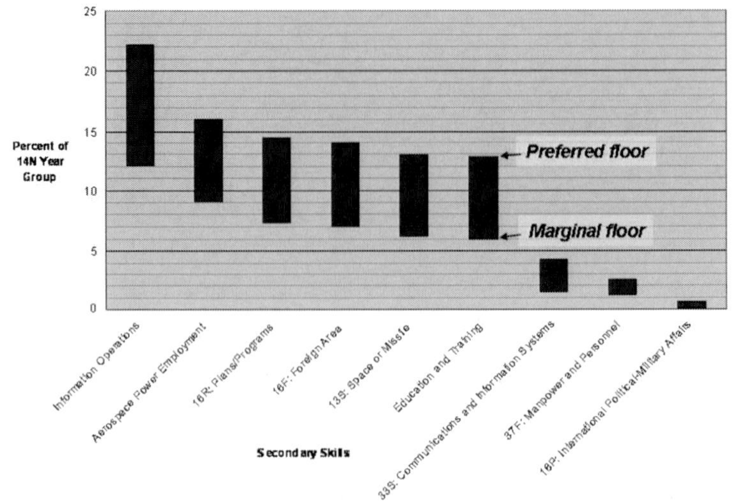

Integrity - Service - Excellence

Slide 22

15W Skill Pairing Targets

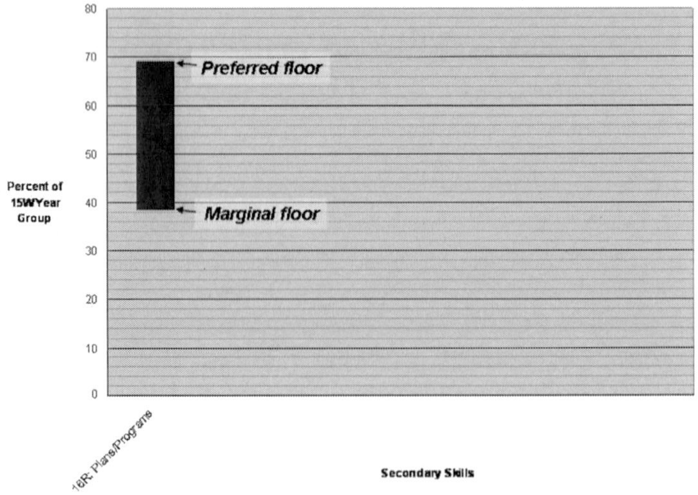

Integrity - Service - Excellence

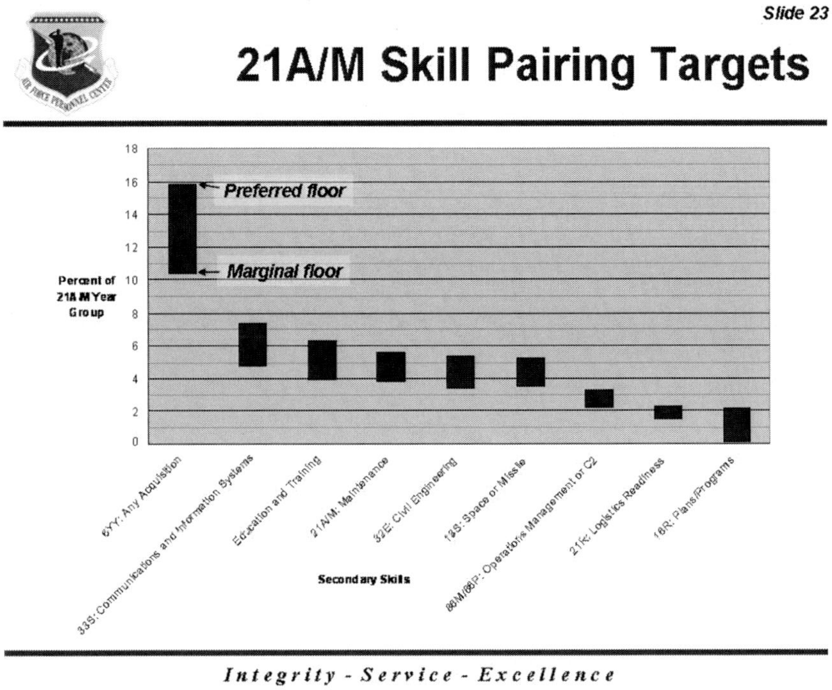
Slide 23
21A/M Skill Pairing Targets
Preferred floor
Marginal floor
Percent of 21A/M Year Group
18
16
14
12
10
8
6
4
2
0
6YY: Any Acquisition
33S: Communications and Information Systems
Education and Training
21A/M: Maintenance
32E: Civil Engineering
13S: Space or Missile
86M/86P: Operations Management or C2
21K: Logistics Readiness
16R: Plans/Programs
Secondary Skills
Integrity - Service - Excellence

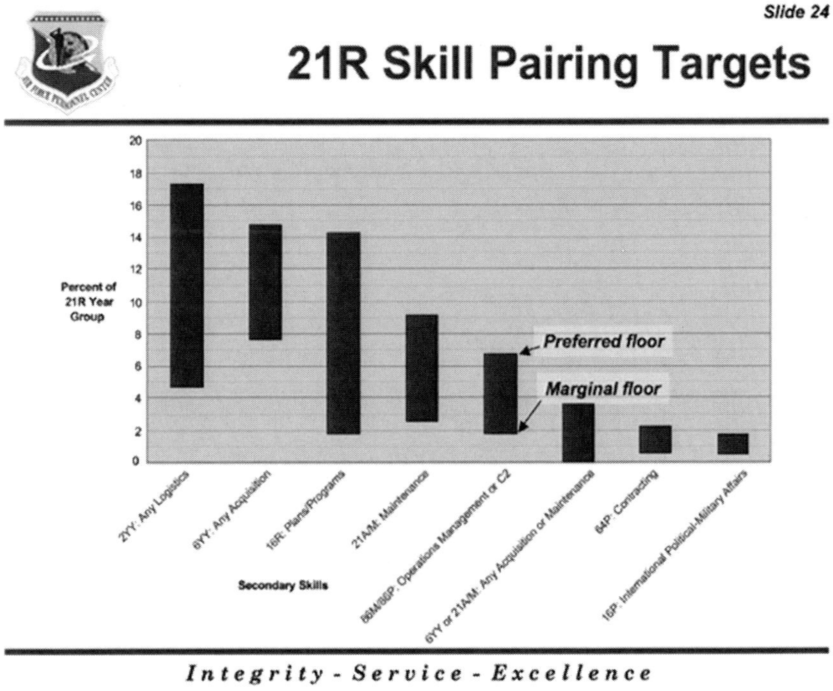
Slide 24
21R Skill Pairing Targets
Preferred floor
Marginal floor
Percent of 21R Year Group
20
18
16
14
12
10
8
6
4
2
0
2YY: Any Logistics
6YY: Any Acquisition
16R: Plans/Programs
21A/M: Maintenance
86M/86P: Operations Management or C2
6YY or 21A/M: Any Acquisition or Maintenance
64P: Contracting
16P: International Political-Military Affairs
Secondary Skills
Integrity - Service - Excellence

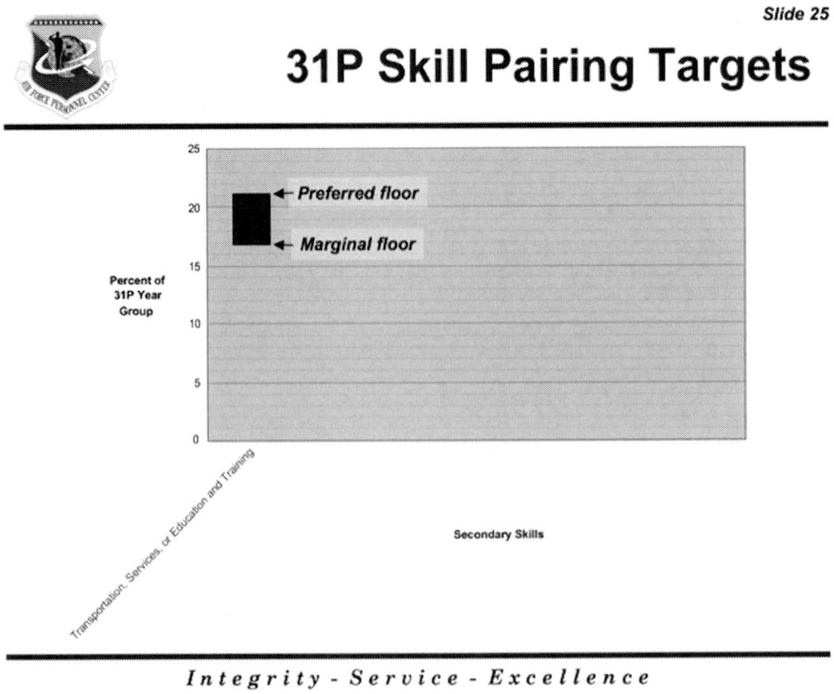
Slide 25
31P Skill Pairing Targets
Preferred floor
Marginal floor
Percent of 31P Year Group
25
20
15
10
5
0
Transportation, Services, or Education and Training
Secondary Skills
Integrity - Service - Excellence

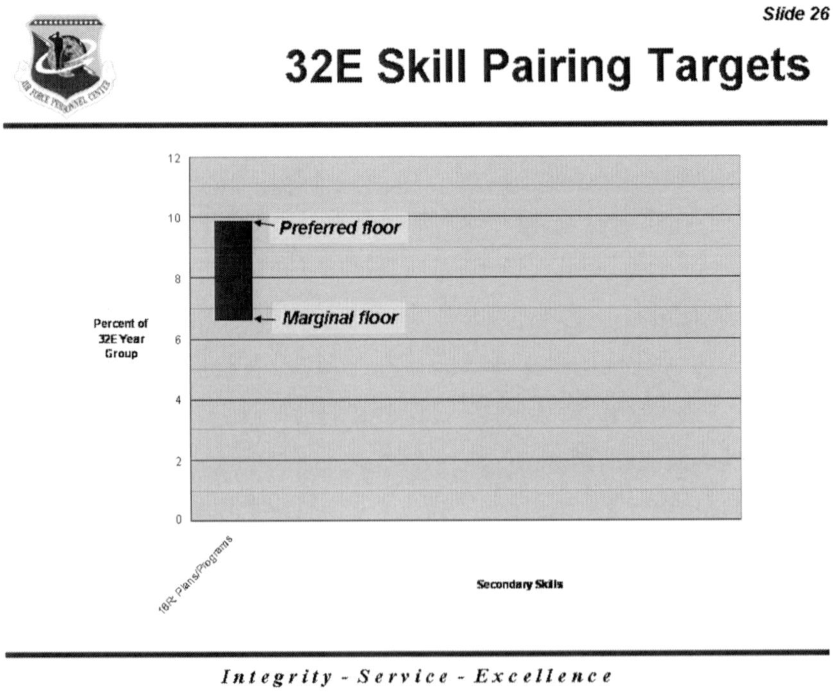
Slide 26
32E Skill Pairing Targets
Preferred floor
Marginal floor
Percent of 32E Year Group
12
10
8
6
4
2
0
16R Plans/Programs
Secondary Skills
Integrity - Service - Excellence

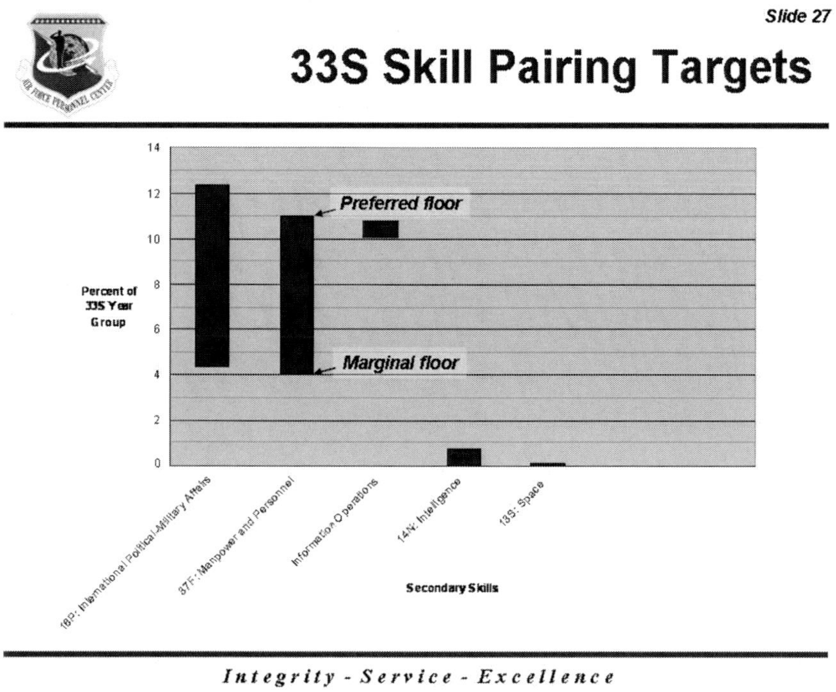
Slide 27
33S Skill Pairing Targets
Percent of 33S Year Group
14
12
10
8
6
4
2
0
Preferred floor
Marginal floor
16P: International Political-Military Affairs
37F: Manpower and Personnel
Information Operations
14N: Intelligence
13S: Space
Secondary Skills
Integrity - Service - Excellence

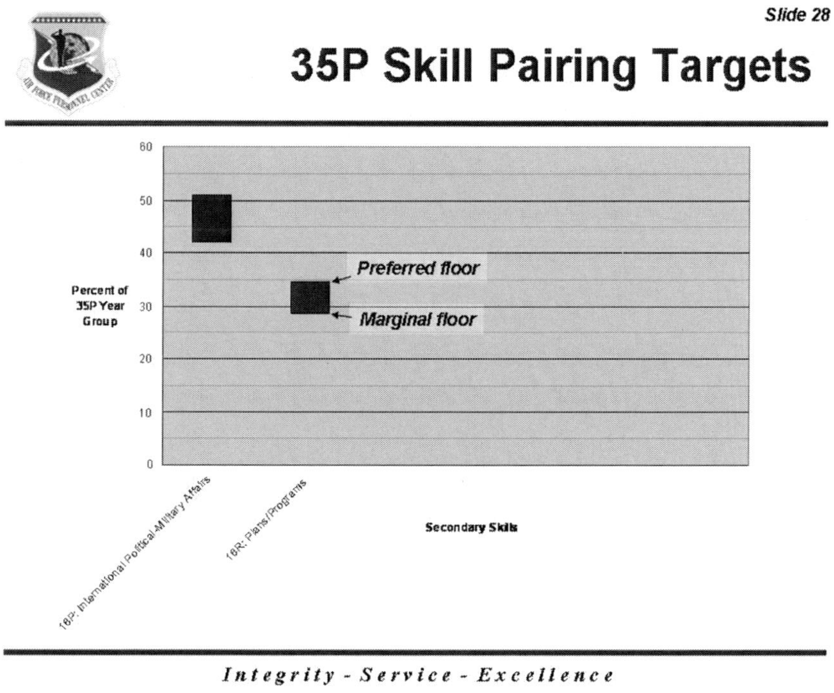
Slide 28
35P Skill Pairing Targets
Percent of 35P Year Group
60
50
40
30
20
10
0
Preferred floor
Marginal floor
16P: International Political-Military Affairs
16R: Plans/Programs
Secondary Skills
Integrity - Service - Excellence

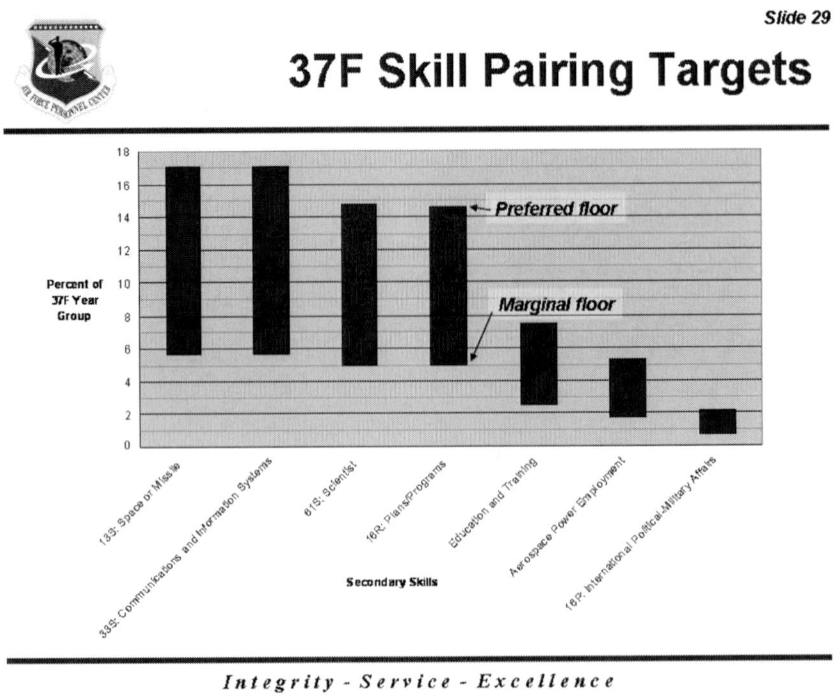
Slide 29
37F Skill Pairing Targets
Percent of 37F Year Group
0
2
4
6
8
10
12
14
16
18
Preferred floor
Marginal floor
13S: Space or Missile
33S: Communications and Information Systems
61S: Scientist
16R: Plans/Programs
Education and Training
Aerospace Power Employment
16P: International Political-Military Affairs
Secondary Skills
Integrity - Service - Excellence

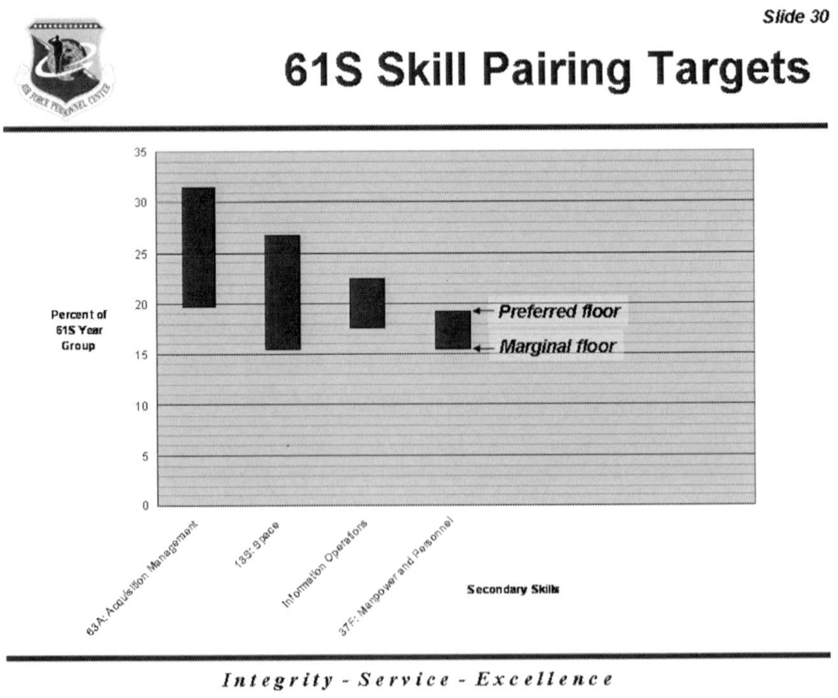
Slide 30
61S Skill Pairing Targets
Percent of 61S Year Group
0
5
10
15
20
25
30
35
Preferred floor
Marginal floor
63A: Acquisition Management
13S: Space
Information Operations
37F: Manpower and Personnel
Secondary Skills
Integrity - Service - Excellence

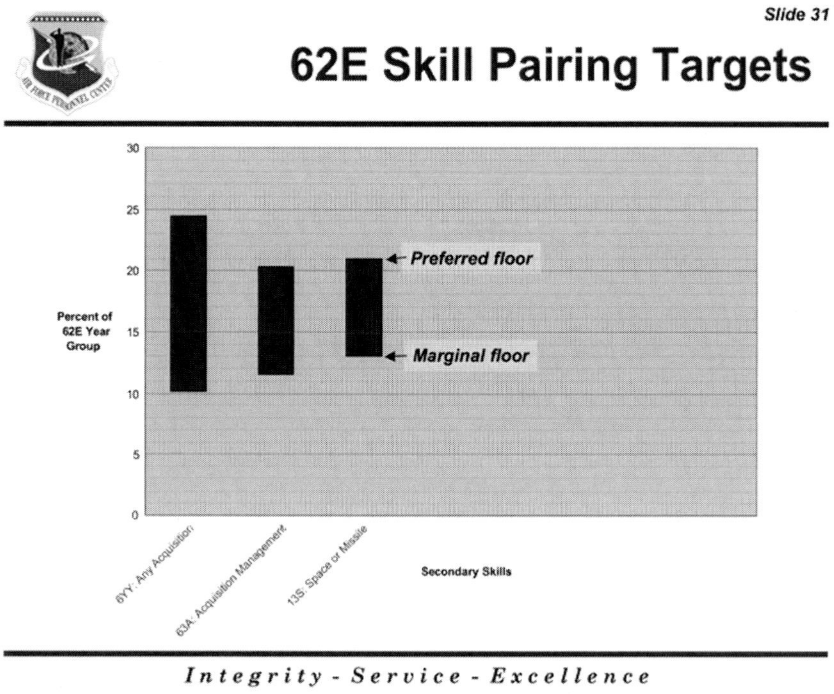
Slide 31
62E Skill Pairing Targets
Percent of 62E Year Group
30
25
20
15
10
5
0
Preferred floor
Marginal floor
6YY: Any Acquisition
63A: Acquisition Management
13S: Space or Missile
Secondary Skills
Integrity - Service - Excellence

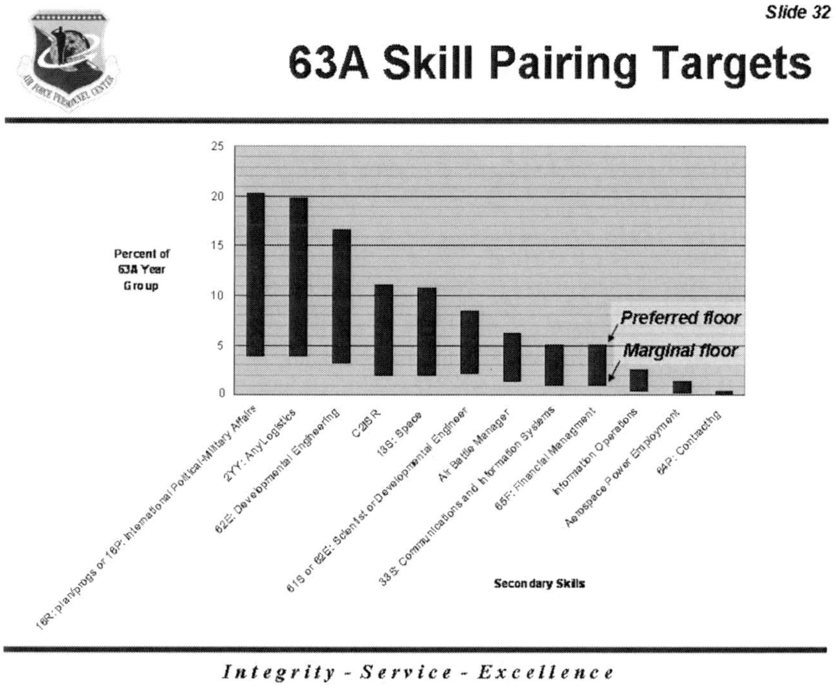
Slide 32
63A Skill Pairing Targets
Percent of 63A Year Group
25
20
15
10
5
0
Preferred floor
Marginal floor
16R: plan/progs or 16P: International Political-Military Affairs
2YY: AnyLogistics
62E: Developmental Engineering
C2ISR
13S: Space
61S or 62E: Scientist or Developmental Engineer
Air Battle Manager
33S: Communications and Information Systems
65F: Financial Managment
Information Operations
Aerospace Power Employment
64P: Contracting
Secondary Skils
Integrity - Service - Excellence

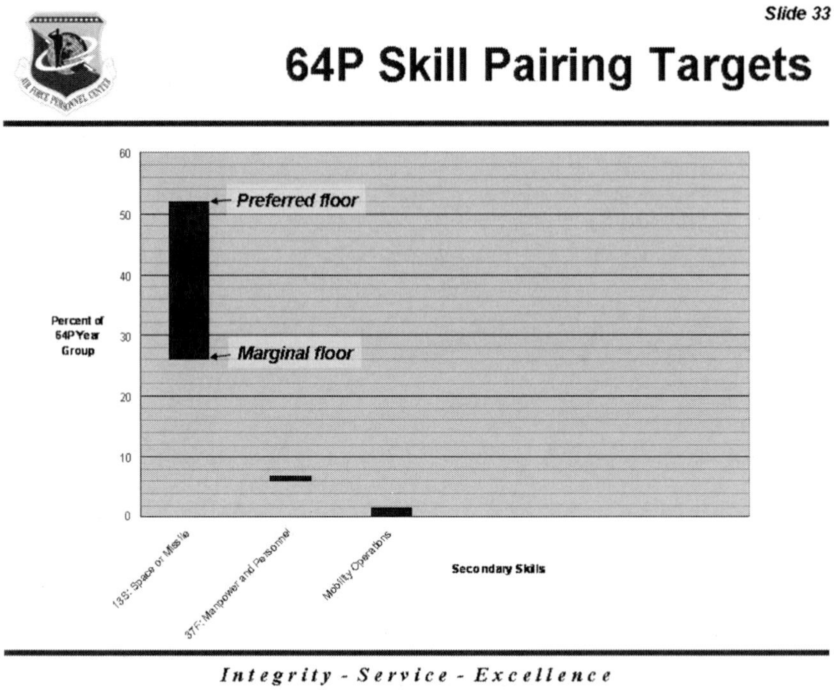
Slide 33
64P Skill Pairing Targets
Percent of 64P Year Group
0
10
20
30
40
50
60
Preferred floor
Marginal floor
13S: Space or Missile
37F: Manpower and Personnel
Mobility Operations
Secondary Skills
Integrity - Service - Excellence

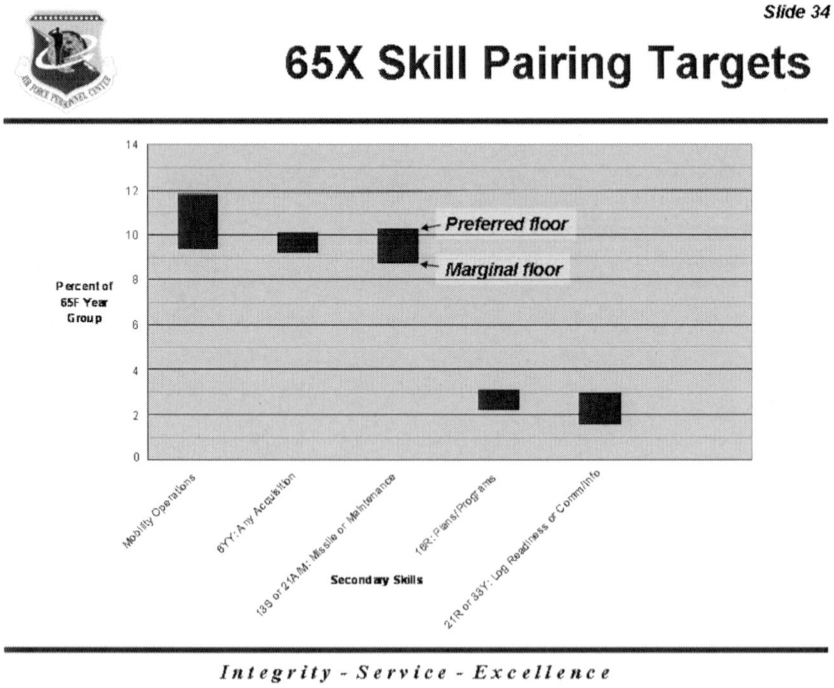
Slide 34
65X Skill Pairing Targets
Percent of 65F Year Group
0
2
4
6
8
10
12
14
Preferred floor
Marginal floor
Mobility Operations
6YY: Any Acquisition
13S or 21A/M: Missile or Maintenance
16R: Plans/Programs
21R or 33Y: Log Readiness or Comm/Info
Secondary Skills
Integrity - Service - Excellence

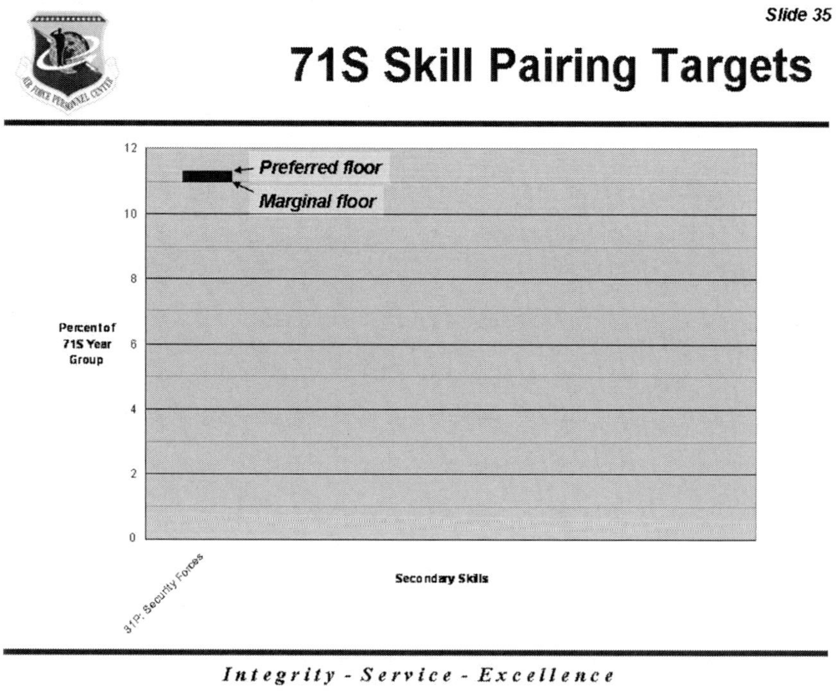
Slide 35
71S Skill Pairing Targets
Preferred floor
Marginal floor
12
10
8
6
4
2
0
Percent of 71S Year Group
31P: Security Forces
Secondary Skills
Integrity - Service - Excellence

References

Brooke, Anthony, David Kendrick, and Alexander Meeraus, *GAMS, Release 2.25, A User's Guide*, Washington, D.C.: The Scientific Press, 1998.

Brauner, Marygail K., Hugh G. Massey, S. Craig Moore, and Darren D. Medlin, *Improving Development and Utilization of U.S. Air Force Intelligence Officers*, Santa Monica, Calif.: RAND Corporation, TR-628-AF, 2009. As of December 23, 2009:
http://www.rand.org/pubs/technical_reports/TR628/

Commission to Assess United States National Security Space Management and Organization, *Report of the Commission to Assess United States National Security Space Management and Organization,* Washington, D.C., January 11, 2001. As of January 29, 2010:
http://www.dod.mil/pubs/space20010111.html

Gabarro, John J., *The Dynamics of Taking Charge,* Boston, Mass.: Harvard Business School Press, 1987.

GlobalSecurity.org, "Aerospace Expeditionary Force (AEF), Air and Space Expeditionary Task Force (ASETF) (Formerly Air Expeditionary Force)," website, 2009. As of July 2009:
http://www.globalsecurity.org/military/agency/usaf/aef-intro.htm

Hanser, Lawrence M., Louis W. Miller, Herbert J. Shukiar, and Bruce O. Newsome, *Developing Senior Navy Leaders: Requirements for Flag Officer Expertise Today and in the Future,* Santa Monica, Calif.: RAND Corporation, MG-618-NAVY, 2008. As of December 31, 2009:
http://www.rand.org/pubs/monographs/MG618/

Hillier, Frederick S., and Gerald J. Lieberman, *Introduction to Operations Research*, 8th ed., New York: McGraw-Hill, 2005.

Leonard, Henry A., J. Michael Polich, Jeffrey D. Peterson, Ronald E. Sortor, and S. Craig Moore, *Something Old, Something New: Army Leader Development in a Dynamic Environment,* Santa Monica, Calif.: RAND Corporation, MG-281-A, 2006. As of December 31, 2009:
http://www.rand.org/pubs/monographs/MG281/

Little, John D.C., "A Proof of the Queueing Formula $L = \lambda W$," *Operations Research,* Vol. 9, 1961, pp. 383–387.

Moore, S. Craig, and Marygail K. Brauner, *Advancing the U.S. Air Force's Force-Development Initiative,* Santa Monica, Calif.: RAND Corporation, MG-545-AF, 2007. As of December 23, 2009:
http://www.rand.org/pubs/monographs/MG545/

Robbert, Albert A., Steve Drezner, John E. Boon, Lawrence M. Hanser, S. Craig Moore, Lynn M. Scott, and Herbert J. Shukiar, *Integrated Planning for the Air Force Senior Leader Workforce: Background and Methods,* Santa Monica, Calif.: RAND Corporation, TR-175-AF, 2005. As of December 23, 2009:
http://www.rand.org/pubs/technical_reports/TR175/

Scott, Lynn M., Steve Drezner, Rachel Rue, and Jesse Reyes, *Certain Competencies May Help Offset Lack of Expertise in Senior Air Force Jobs,* Santa Monica, Calif.: RAND Corporation, RB-235-AF, 2007a. As of December 23, 2009:
http://www.rand.org/pubs/research_briefs/RB235/

———, *Compensating for Incomplete Domain Knowledge,* Santa Monica, Calif.: RAND Corporation, DB-517-AF, 2007b. As of December 23, 2009:
http://www.rand.org/pubs/documented_briefings/DB517/

Space Professional Development, website, 2006. As of February 20, 2010: http://www.acq.osd.mil/SpaceCadre/SpaceCadreHome.html

U.S. Air Force, *Leadership and Force Development,* AFDD 1-1, February 18, 2006.

———, "Force Development Flight Plan" (DRAFT), January 18, 2007.

———, *Executing Total Force Development,* AFI 36-2640, December 16, 2008.

Vernez, Georges, S. Craig Moore, Steven Martino, and Jeffrey Yuen, *Improving the Development and Utilization of Air Force Space and Missile Officers,* Santa Monica, Calif.: RAND Corporation, MG-382-AF, 2006. As of December 23, 2009: http://www.rand.org/pubs/monographs/MG382/